SPARKLE
AND
SHINE

How to Create a Joyful, Radiant Spiritual Journey

Thank you for supporting VT!
Love, Victoria

VICTORIA M. TEAGUE

ISBN: 978-1-64746-212-3

Library of Congress Control Number: 2020905467

Printed in Suwannee, Georgia, USA by Victoria Teague

Edited by Sallie W. Boyles, WriteLady.com

The publisher has strived to be as accurate and complete as possible in the creation of this book.

The advice and strategies found within may not be suitable for every situation. This work is sold with the understanding that neither the author nor the publisher is held responsible for the results accrued from the advice in this book.

For more information, visit www.Victorias-Friends.com.

For bulk book orders, contact Victoria Teague at victoriasfriends@msn.com.

Acknowledgements

I am so grateful that we all operate with many gifts and talents. This writing project exists because of the collaborative work of my writer's tribe. Special thanks to Diana M. Needham, founder of Business Book Partners, my publishing and launch queen! I have the vision and she's into the details—a perfect match! Thank you, Diana, for making my books beautiful and for all the efforts to make my launch a huge success.

Also, a huge thank you to Sallie Boyles, my editor and dear friend. Sallie, you make my words beautiful and bring our book projects to the next level. I cannot express how grateful I am to have you as my editor. You make writing a JOY!

We did it, team!

Dedication

This book is dedicated to three special ladies, my sisters and family in Christ, who cared enough to spend three hours on a fall afternoon that changed all of eternity for me, and the many others whose lives will be healed, touched, and set free in Jesus Christ.

Let's all roar like the Lion of Judah, ladies, until the trumpet blows!

Contents

Introduction

People ask me to speak all over my community in all types of settings. I'll never forget the time I spoke at county fair to raise money for a group that helped special needs children. After gladly accepting, I did wonder about the type of outfit I should wear and chose to dress casually. Most who presented had the same thought, but a moment of crisis would demonstrate that attitudes mattered more than attire.

On the big day, I arrived as the other speakers were showing up, and one lady immediately caught my attention. She was dressed up in high heels and wearing a diamond-and-ruby necklace and matching bracelet. I remember thinking, *Wow, she's really decked out for an outdoor event!*

Given my gift of gab (I never meet a stranger) and her friendly personality, she and I easily struck up a conversation. While chatting, we also thought to find a ladies' room before it was time to speak. Our only option were port-a-potties—oh yeah, outhouses! The accommodations wouldn't have been so terrible if my new friend's keys hadn't fallen from her pocket in the process of her using the facilities.

You guessed it! They landed smack in the middle of the hole. Never a dull moment! Having no luck upon asking around for help or figuring out a better way to retrieve her keys, she finally stuck her arm down the lovely hole of slush and poop.

I'll never forget the look on her face as she emerged from that port-a-potty, dangling the keys. No longer sparkling, her beautiful ruby-and-diamond bracelet was covered in poop. What a sight! Thankfully, we found soap and water to wash her hands, arms, bracelet, and keys. Sparkling once again, she delivered her speech like a pro and later drove herself home. I was so proud of my new friend. What a speaking event!

Ladies, what do we do when the world slings poop on our jewels? Do we give up, or do we stand and fight? Do we let it roll off our backs or defeat us?

Sparkle and Shine is all about how to sparkle in a world that dulls our shine.

We're all meant to shine. Maybe that's why we are so drawn to gemstones. Which one is your favorite? How about diamonds?

It's hard to believe that diamonds—the stars of the most lavish jewelry in the world—are made purely of carbon atoms. The stones are produced as those atoms lock. This takes place about a hundred miles beneath the earth's surface under extreme pressure and heat, over a long time period. Diamonds mined today began forming one to three billion years ago.

When found, however, diamonds aren't sparkling the way we're used to seeing them in jewelry. They must be cut and polished expertly to maximize the three secrets to their natural brilliance: reflection, refraction, and dispersion.

Reflection describes the way a diamond shines after light hits its surface and bounces back.

Light also travels through the diamond, where angles within the stone scatter and break up the light. *Refraction*, which refers to the movement and distribution of light, creates the diamond's unique sparkle.

Diamonds are also prisms that break up light and emit rainbows. The term for that colorful display is *dispersion*.

Believe or not, diamonds also have a dark side—many, in fact. Refraction and dispersion produce light and dark areas based upon where light hits the diamond. It would seem that any amount of darkness would make a diamond appear less brilliant, but the opposite is true. Consider how a candle flame always looks brighter in a dark room than it does in a well-lit space. The reason is contrast. A diamond could shine without contrast, but it would look significantly less impressive to the eye.

The cut also determines just how brilliant a diamond appears. If too deep or too shallow, the diamond won't reflect light optimally. For several reasons, diamond

cutters must be highly skilled experts. Besides deter-
mining the thickness, they use the natural properties
of the diamond—including its size, shape, and intricate
angles—to maximize the stone's brilliance. The overall
shape must be pleasing, too. Therefore, another factor
affecting its beauty is symmetry, which results from cut-
ting and shaping the facets of a diamond evenly. Also,
if the facets aren't perfectly symmetrical, the light won't
refract properly.

Clarity impacts a diamond's shine as well. Whether
blemishes on the surface or inclusions on the inside, a
stone's imperfections interfere with light. That's why a
diamond's clarity influences its value. As a result, the
final step of polishing a diamond to smooth over the
surface and remove any exterior blemishes is quite
important.

Clearly, such beauty doesn't come quickly or easily,
which is why diamonds are valuable and cherished.

What can we take from this lesson about diamonds?

Zechariah 9 in the Bible says, "We will sparkle in his
land like jewels in a crown."

We are all valuable and cherished gemstones. Yet we
all wonder how to sparkle in a world that dulls our shine.
Like the diamond, our spiritual journeys will include
some dull and dark phases that precede the sparkle and
shine. Even if we don't start out feeling valuable and
cherished, by digging deeply and looking closely, we
find that we are.

This book uses the principles that cause a diamond to sparkle to reveal three remarkable ways in which we acquire the ability to shine:

1. Reflection: Use meditation to produce thoughts, ideas, opinions, and remarks.
   As we reflect on our Heavenly Father and look to Him, He gives us thoughts, ideas, and opinions that make us shine brightly. He makes us stand out!

2. Refraction: Understand that a ray of light or wave of energy is *broken* when deflected or turned, producing the magnificence of a rainbow.
   We shine when we embrace our brokenness, trials, U-turns, exits, and detours, and refuse to jump ship. The difficult and unexpected trials are what cause us to shine brilliantly and colorfully.

3. Dispersion: Scatter light.
   As we embrace all that our Heavenly Father has for us, we turn back and scatter the light to others.

Through each one, our private time with the Lord is *key*. That's our entry point. Let's reflect on our Father. Give Him our broken and wounded places. Stay with Him on the journey in the midst of the unexpected bumps, turns, and twists. Stay with the difficult seasons. Our trials serve a purpose, so let's not run from them.

Let's stay where we are and make it fruitful. When we stay in that place, we learn more. We grow more. We become more. We do more.

God is turning up the pressure and the heat on us so that He can bring forth diamonds. Not just any diamond—diamonds that sparkle and shine.

1

Secret Power

> *"The more we let God take us over, the more truly ourselves we become— because he made us. He invented us. He invented all the different people that you and I were intended to be... It is when I turn to Christ, when I give up myself to his personality, that I first begin to have a real personality of my own."*
>
> **– C. S. Lewis**

I was eight months pregnant. I didn't believe I had the energy or emotional reserves to stay at a villa with eight other ladies for an entire weekend. My friend coerced me to go. Perhaps, deep down, I knew that my church's annual women's spiritual retreat at Callaway Gardens would be an amazing experience.

Upon arriving, I found that I knew a couple of women in our villa but not everyone. That had me thinking, *If these ladies only knew about my past and who I was, they would not want to be rooming with me.* I was nervous and exhausted but wanted to hear from God.

As we unpacked our belongings, a lady popped her head in our room to say hello. After she left, one of my roommates commented, "Oh, she's the perfect one. You know, the lady who never gossips, is always on time, always put together, and her children look perfect, too!" She went on to say that the lady never gets ruffled, always loves from her heart — a loyal friend, wife, and mother. I felt myself shrinking back and feeling a little insecure.

Have you been there? I was afraid that people were going to find out about me, and I would not measure up.

I'd accepted Christ and kept my past between my husband Jeff and me. Jeff knew my story, he loved me, and that was enough for me. I was still coming out of so much trauma and had serious trust issues.

When I was in high school, I struggled with so much tragedy. My sister died of cancer when I was fifteen, and at sixteen, I suffered a rape from a trusted date. I found myself grabbing for safety, power, and excitement in all the wrong places. Seeking desperately for happiness in all the worldly forms, I turned to romantic relationships to feel special, only to feel rejected each and every time. As I turned to drugs, alcohol, and sex to numb all my pain, I shut out the small, still, inner voice of God that I had once known. I turned my back on God and pummeled into a dark spiral of drugs, stripping, and even prostitution at the end of the eleven-year descent.

One morning, having hit rock bottom with addiction and shame, I remembered when I was five years old and my Aunt Evelyn had taken me to church. I remembered the light feeling I'd felt as I learned about prayers and a God who loved me deeply. I remembered the love. As the drugs and alcohol were wearing off, I got on my knees and prayed. "God, help me?" I asked.

At that moment, I looked up, and seeing the sunlight was coming through the window in the most unique way, I remembered the love. The connection was there despite all my worldly shenanigans. This universal love touched me deeply, and as I cried out, it set off a ricochet of events in my favor.

My Aunt Evelyn had taught me so much as a child. The seeds of love were sown, and the connection to the irresistible love of God was still there. By the help of a precious woman and her family, I made it out of that horrible season, and I promised that I would never let go of my commitment to God and His love ever again. That was three decades ago. I've now been a Christian for thirty years. I've been on a spiritual journey, strengthening and nurturing that love ever sense. My relationship to God and His irresistible love is the most important thing in my life. Without it, I lose my power, purpose, calling, and connection to love.

When I went to the retreat, I was at the beginning of this journey. Insecure and afraid of what others might think, I held onto God, Jeff's love, and the few friends I had, including the friend who'd brought me there.

As the music played and the sessions started, I felt so much love. And what did I do then, as I do now, when feeling loved? Of course, I ran my mouth! We were all chatting and sharing our stories, and it was amazing. I felt connected and loved—even from the "perfect" women attending. Not only did I feel connected, but I also felt bonded with them all.

Driving home after an action-packed weekend of music, spiritual feelings, connecting, and sharing, I had the thought, *Oh, Jeff is going to be upset because I shared so much.* Yet, it was a huge weight off my soul and spirit to get those dark secrets out.

The friend who'd convinced me to attend the retreat and I both stayed connected with the other women, including the "perfect one," whose name is Carolyn. As she and I got to know each other, Carolyn shared how she was actually feeling that first night in Callaway Gardens.

"As I arrived at the retreat," Carolyn confided, "I noticed all these women grouped together, chatting about one thing and then another. Most of the ladies had smiles on their faces. I wore a smile, too, but it was not a reflection of what was happening in my heart. My smile and bubbly countenance formed the mask I'd put on to avoid being found out. What I really wanted to do was run and hide.

"On the outside," she continued, "I was a well-put-together church mom with trendy shoes and snappy jeans. On the inside, I was a cowering little girl, afraid that people would discover the real me. *What's wrong with me? Why don't I feel the joy these other women feel? What holds me back from experiencing the confidence and assurance they feel? Why do they seem so happy? Where is the abundant life Jesus talked about? I feel like I'm wandering around in a maze to find a way out of these feelings of inadequacy.*"

Carolyn went on to say, "The problem was: I was stuck. Yes, I had professed Jesus as my Lord and Savior. I knew Christ set me free, but, honestly, I could not tell you what He set me free from. I knew if I died, I would not burn in hell, but I had a nagging feeling that something was missing. What?"

This is the perfect church chick? I was shocked.

Stunned, I continued to listen. "My early years in the faith were filled with wonder and expectancy," she said, "but somewhere along the line, I settled into being a good church girl—a Bible study mom who pitched my tent in the church and waved at all other well-mannered believers doing the same. As I stayed in the church camp, my spiritual walk became more like a crawl. I started feeling disappointed in myself and a sense of guilt in my time with God. I showed up at the retreat asking myself, *Is this all there is?*"

So, there we were, two women who were total opposites yet equally insecure. I went to the retreat having left a dark world of rebellion and promiscuity. Carolyn went having become a burned-out "church chick." I'd looked at her and thought, *Wow, she's so perfect. If I could only be like her.* At the same time, Carolyn had looked at me and thought, *Wow, she's so hungry for the things of God and so passionate about Christ, if I could only be like her.*

Little did we know we were about to merge smack in the center with Jesus and a huge revelation of His love!

When you get hundreds of ladies together for a weekend of music and spiritual feedings, God shows up. Our event was no exception. God showed up and blew our socks off. We all received a huge revelation of His amazing and irresistible love.

In sharing, we found out we were not alone. Among us were many Victorias and Carolyns, and not any of us needed to run and hide. A deep, deep bond formed within our villa, and the same occurred among the other groups. The sharing of laughter, joy, tears, and love spread throughout the retreat.

While praying over this book and the title, I started reading about the elements that make diamonds shine. I then looked back on how we'd spent the retreat reflecting on Jesus. Making the connection provided an exciting revelation.

I often find that a simple dictionary definition highlights a point and adds perspective, such as this one given by Merriam-Webster for *reflection*: "a thought, idea, or opinion formed, or a remark made as a result of meditation." As we reflect on our Heavenly Father and look to Him, He gives us thoughts, ideas, and opinions that make us shine brightly. He makes us stand out!

One of our sessions during the retreat focused on Moses **Exodus 34:29-35**:

> When Moses came down from Mount Sinai with the two tablets of the Testimony in his hands, he was not aware that his face was radiant because he had spoken with the LORD. When Aaron and all the Israelites saw Moses, his face was radiant, and they were afraid to come near him.
>
> But Moses called to them; so Aaron and all the leaders of the community came back to him, and he spoke to them.
>
> Afterward all the Israelites came near him, and he gave them all the commands the LORD had given him on Mount Sinai. When Moses finished speaking to them, he put a veil over his face.
>
> But whenever he entered the LORD's presence to speak with him, he removed the veil until he came out. And when he came out and told the Israelites what he had been commanded,

> they saw that his face was radiant. Then Moses
> would put the veil back over his face until he
> went in to speak with the LORD.

I loved reading that Moses's face glowed after spending time speaking with God, and the fact that I was pregnant with my daughter Hannah at the time really brought it home. Everyone was telling me I had the pregnant glow, even though I did not feel like it. However, I could imagine that Moses must have been pregnant with God's glory. His face was radiant, glowing.

Radiate is another descriptive word to mean sparkle, glisten, and shine. If we want to shine, let's follow Moses's example by shutting the world out and spending time with God.

After the retreat, I went on to birth Victoria's Friends, a sex-trafficking ministry. We go to the strip clubs and prostituted areas of Atlanta to reach ladies who are still stumbling in the darkness. Carolyn got involved with an adoption ministry and adopted two beautiful young girls from Asia. Another attendee started a group for women with eating disorders. Those are only a few examples of how we went out into the community, shining our lights brightly.

Who among us is shining brightly to our family, friends, and community? As I speak all over the nation, I continually meet women who are burned out. How about each of us? Are we shining brightly to a lost and dying world?

I use what the retreat revealed and ignited in a diverse group of women to demonstrate that God is no respecter of persons. This is for us all. If He will take me, a former stripper and prostitute, He will surely take you. Whether you've been in rebellion (like I had been) or bent on rules and goodness (like Carolyn was), it makes no difference. The secret power is for us all.

Here's the formula:

- Speak with the Lord daily: We must follow Moses's example, realizing that when he came down from the mountain, his face was radiant because he'd spoken with the Lord.
- Be a light reflector: As we wait on the light of heaven to dawn, we are the light reflectors (2 Corinthians 3:18).
- Get face to face with Jesus: Having a heart connection with Jesus, not a head knowledge, allows us to shine.

Again, being in tune with God is not an exclusive privilege for the elite. We were created to be a light to those around us—not to point out the darkness that blinds us from the truth. God is light, and where there is light, there is vision. Where there is vision, there is hope and recovery of sight. Where there is sight, there is revelation. With a revelation of how God does things, we learn to live in sync with Him.

Reflection after spending time with God alone and spending time together in community is the secret. We stand out by reflecting the light of God, which we see in the person of Jesus Christ, to a lost, dark, and dying world. That's how we sparkle and shine.

We are all bright lights, so let's go, ladies! Let's shine!

2

Rough Diamonds Are Getting All the Attention

Someone somewhere is depending on your doing what God has called you to do.

– Unknown

Shawn was taken from Chicago to California at seven years old by the only man that he knew as his father. Even though his parents had gone through a divorce that gave custody to his mother, during a scheduled visitation, his father had tricked Shawn into going on a trip with him. Eight years later, after the final blow of his father choking and beating him, Shawn gained the courage to go to his next-door neighbors for help. They knew that the father, a former marine, had been roughing up the boy for years, so they were eager to assist Shawn in calling his mother and coordinating his escape. They got him to the airport without the abuser's knowledge.

Several years later, on a Christmas Eve, my daughter and I were meeting Shawn for the first time at the church. I was a little nervous. My pastor had called me a week before to explain the reason, which he said was "a little different." Not a single mom, the individual was a single dad in the sex industry who needed help. Could Victoria's Friends assist? I responded that of course, we'd love to. We had two Christmas scholarships—financial assistance—left to give. I wondered what we were getting into and how Shawn would respond to us.

Have you ever had a knowingness that you were supposed to help someone? My daughter and I did upon meeting Shawn and his son. The minute we saw them, we felt an instant kinship and fell in love.

Shawn later shared the rest of his story on a podcast for Victoria's Friends.

> It was quite a reunion for my mother and me. For one thing, I'd left sunny California, landed in Chicago in the middle of winter, and jumped off the plane at fourteen years old in a tank top and shorts. *Br-r-r-r!* She never thought she would see me again. I was taken from her at seven years old, and what she saw getting off the airplane was a 6'2" teenager.

Shawn's mother and his stepdad worked quickly to repair the broken relationship. Both mother and grandmother, two spiritual, godly women, had loved him and prayed for him his entire life. His family had rallied for him. They helped him get in college, and Shawn graduated. In contrast, Shawn never liked the man who'd said he was his father. Years later, at his mother's funeral, he learned the man was not even his dad. (To this day, Shawn has nothing to do with him.)

After graduating from college, Shawn entered law enforcement and served on the security team when Atlanta hosted the Summer Olympics in 1996. In the midst of the festivities, a bomb went off at Olympic Park in downtown Atlanta, where it killed one and injured over a hundred others. Shawn was part of a team that traveled to the North Georgia mountains and beyond on the manhunt. With a bounty placed on the bomber, all involved in the search were under tremendous pressure to find the killer. On top of that, law enforcement officials had to deal with unwelcoming mountain residents, who would appear on their front porches with their guns in hand. Shawn confessed that the movie *Deliverance*, a story about a disturbing encounter between men from the city and inhabitants of rural Georgia, entered his thoughts.

As he recalled his fears, I had a hard time imagining anything that could frighten Shawn. He's a big man. My head doesn't reach his shoulders. At Victoria's Friends, we fondly refer to him as "Shrek." Despite his towering, fearsome appearance, he has a kind heart and loves everyone.

Although his character didn't seem to fit the sex industry, he used part of the podcast to explain how he'd entered that world.

> I was working a security job when I met a man who owned the world's largest hotels and casinos. That's when I stepped into that dark world. He had ties to the strip clubs and mafia, and for about eight years, I was his personal bodyguard. We traveled around the world, where he had hotels, casinos, construction, and we did a large portion of our business deals at the strip clubs. It was a season of highs and lows and traveling with strippers. I took care of the ladies and transported them as they entertained and took care of the businessmen. The ladies all called me "Big Shawn."
>
> Then I got a dancer pregnant. I did not want to believe it or have anything to do with it. About three weeks before he was born, I went back to her and stood in the delivery room, watching her give birth. When he came out, the world stopped. Everything went silent. That beautiful boy was mine. I held my boy

and told him, "I love you, and I'll stay by your side for the rest of your life."

My life of breaking kneecaps was gone the minute I laid eyes on my son. Roughing folks up just didn't fit with changing diapers. After two months, my girlfriend went back to the lifestyle of stripping. She decided she did not want to be a mom, so I got full custody of my son. I married another lady. It did not work out, and she left and never came back. So, I have full custody of my younger one, too.

Shawn's life is a miracle. A good guy, he made decisions that trapped him in a bad world, and then stepped up to the plate as a single dad. "I love my boys and want to be there every day in every way," is his heart's cry. Wow... what a hero!

His story is a fragment of what it's like to operate Victoria's Friends. Like many who call the hotline, Shawn had hit hard times financially. We responded by granting a scholarship that took the pressure off and allowed him to make it through a tight season.

Not long after the podcast, Valentine's Day arrived. Our Valentine's outreach for Victoria's Friends is always an exciting time. Typically, we're loading my car up with beautiful soaps, spa balls, and other treats in pink, red, and lavender holiday bags for the dancers at the strip clubs. The most important ingredient we add is love. We all realize that they almost never get anything free. That's why it's so meaningful for us to go into the dressing rooms of their clubs and share and chat and just love up on them. We let them know we have a support group and many resources. A scholarship package is also available if they are interested in transitioning out of the sex industry.

We use the back entrance of the strip clubs, which always welcome us with open arms. Since we provide a way out for the ladies, you would think the managers would object to us. Ironically, they are happy that we look out for their ladies. We raise employee morale.

On the Valentine's outreach following the podcast, the Victoria's Friends team was chatting with the house mom of a club—the lady on staff who assists the dancers backstage. While we were talking, she asked if the Shawn I'd interviewed happened to be Big Shawn. (Many of the ladies and house moms are Facebook fans, so they would have had the opportunity to listen.) I thanked her for listening and played it on my phone to affirm that yes, he was Big Shawn. She'd thought so but still exclaimed, "No way!"

I played the podcast in the dressing room so the dancers could hear Big Shawn, and as the word spread among them, a large group gathered. The dancers were so glued to the show that the bouncer came looking for them. "Ladies," he yelled, "there are customers on the floor. What are you listening to?" Upon hearing Big Shawn's voice, he also started listening to the gospel message, raw and coming from one of their own. God in His great love had wrapped His arms around one of their very own friends.

Later that night, I noticed that the bouncer was all over our website and Facebook fan page. I stood back from it and prayed, *God, what's up with this?* The bouncers rarely had anything to do with us when we came in with our bags and baskets. Usually, they were not interested. Through God, Shawn had opened the door, and he has since joined Victoria's Friends in helping us reach the men involved in the industry. From seeing that one bouncer's interest, I took the opportunity to invite him to church.

Shawn's story mirrored that of Saul, who became the Apostle Paul.

Shawn admitted that the entire time he was with the mob, he'd known better. Why? He had a praying grandmother and mother. Shawn's goodness—his love for his children and concern for others—comes through the love of Christ, passed on from Mom and Grandma. All the violence came from a man Shawn had thought was his dad but wasn't. Being treated that way led Shawn to hurt people. He was violent. However, the Word prayed over him by his mother and grandmother was operating in his life. As Shawn has expressed, "They were by my side every day." The Word of God never runs dry.

I just know Shawn's mother and grandmother were praying when he signed up his sons to play baseball. Shawn admitted to his being a "loudmouth" as he watched his sons' games from the stands. Besides yelling, he sometimes cursed. All the while, a sweet and somewhat quiet couple who had a son in the game as well would sit not too far from him. When Shawn ended up being invited to church by a man who'd hired him, he said his jaw hit the ground upon seeing the same couple come out on the stage and preach. Thinking back on the foul words that had come out of his mouth in front of them, he wanted to crawl under his pew.

The couple, Johnson and Summer, are senior pastors. Even more shocking to Shawn was soft-spoken Pastor Johnson's ability to deliver such a powerful, riveting message. I agree! As Shawn has expressed, "He can preach, and, man, he preaches with power, proclaiming the gospels in a very unique way." His animated demeanor and the energy in his delivery grabbed Shawn, making him connect to the messages.

After the service, Shawn went up and apologized for his mouth at the games and found out how easily relatable Johnson and Summer could be. They've not only become key figures in Shawn's journey, but have loved him and his boys deeply, including the three in cookouts at their home and treating them like family. Through their relationship, Shawn decided to accept Christ. He was baptized. Pastors Summer and Johnson were also the same who introduced Shawn to Victoria's Friends.

This is what it is to be in a community with the bride of Christ: rallying for one another in love and fellowship. No other ties compare to the love, belonging, and commitment felt within a spiritual family.

The love and prayers that have enveloped Shawn remind me of the mother-of-pearl clouds that Jeff and I had the privilege of spotting when we were on an Alaskan cruise. The formations are rare, mostly seen in the high latitudes near the Arctic Circle—for example, Scandinavia, Iceland, Alaska, and Northern Canada—near dawn or after sunset. They appeared in the sky for us a little after sunset.

Once you see mother-of-pearl clouds you never forget. Their high altitudes—eighty thousand feet above the earth—and composition—uniform crystals of ice—allow them to reflect the light of the sun, creating a breathtaking, wavy rainbow effect, when the land below is dark. Seeing them, I felt as if God were showing off in the sky.

Ah… we now have diamonds *and* pearls.

Remember, refraction and dispersion create light and dark areas in the diamond. The dark adds the magic by magnifying the intensity of the shine. The height and the altitude create the pearls in the sky. (Rising and reaching the heights, they reflect the sun.) Pearls and diamonds!

Those mother-of-pearl clouds portray how the prayers offered by Shawn's mother and grandmother became forces that lifted and pushed him to higher places so he could reflect the sun. The imagery vividly portrays the power of prayers, especially when they come from the heart of a mother and grandmother.

Like diamonds and pearls, those loving women shined brightly, reflecting the Son. With a spirit of light that cuts and turns through the darkness, they opened up love in a big way for Shawn and his boys. They further paved the way for the father and his two sons to meet divine connections that would direct them in their spiritual journey to Christ.

In his interview with me, Shawn hadn't shared half the trauma he'd been through. Any rational person who hears his full story cannot explain his ability to survive so much without prayers that produce miracles. With all I learned about his past, I had to get in my prayer closet for about an hour after we did that podcast.

Can you pick out the diamonds in this story? Let's remember that refraction and dispersion create light and dark areas in a diamond. Dark is the magic element. Why? It magnifies the intensity of the shine.

We can see Shawn's mother and grandmother as the diamonds. Their prayers were the light bending into darkness. With their loving prayers, they never let go of Shawn.

While his grandmother is still alive, no doubt sheltering Shawn and the boys with her prayers, Shawn's mother had passed away by the time Shawn and Victoria's Friends crossed paths. Seeing that he had been beaten down to a pulp, I prayed and asked the Holy Spirit how I could best help him. God responded with a question: *What does a good mother do?* Of course, she feeds and cares for her kids. I saw then that one of my roles was to be a mother to Shawn and a grandmother to the boys.

Oftentimes, when there's a need in a person's life, God brings someone to fill in the gaps until the person is healed and free from the trauma that becomes paralyzing. It's unbelievable what some people survive in this world.

Ladies, we are called to be God's leading roles. Are you being still enough and praying and asking God what He wants you to do with each opportunity or relationship He brings into your life?

Through prayer, we see that each of us has a role, whether it's mother, grandmother, friend, or prayer warrior. Our prayers just might save someone's life. My Aunt Evelyn prayed for me for eleven years while I was in rebellion. I'm sure it was God's grace and her prayers that kept me alive on many occasions. We are called to carry the light and let it bend throughout the darkness surrounding our loved ones, friends, and family.

Are you praying fervently and often for your children?

We can shine our light in two ways:

- By being still and praying and asking God what role we are to play in the relationships that come into our life
- By praying for our children

Let's shine our light into the darkness, ladies. Let it shine.

"I am reminded of your sincere faith, a faith that dwelt first in your grandmother Lois and your mother Eunice and now, I am sure, dwells in you as well"

2 Timothy 1:5

3

The God of Bright Lights

"For You light my lamp; The LORD my God
illumines my darkness"

Psalm 18:28

She sat as patiently as possible in the gynecologist's waiting room. Nervous about what the doctor might discover, Boudhsalinh glanced over a mix of magazines and brochures on a nearby table. The bold type, VICTORIA'S FRIENDS, on one of the brochures stood out. Boudhsalinh grabbed it just as the nurse called her name. Later that day, she called Victoria's Friends' hotline, curious to see how they could help.

Marlene Gaskill, who has since gone to be with the Lord, had been working the hotline that day. She'd quickly become a mother figure to Boudhsalinh.

Boudhsalinh's family had immigrated to the U.S. after surviving the Killing Fields of Cambodia, where the genocide and burial of more than a million people took place from 1975 to 1979 at the hands of the country's former communist regime, the Khmer Rouge. Leading their escape that started out on foot, her father had to carry Boudhsalinh, only three years old, on his back. Only a miracle could explain how Boudhsalinh's family made it out alive.

As she grew up in the States, Boudhsalinh had to carry her weight. Becoming a stripper and a prostitute allowed her to earn money for her family. They lived in poverty, and it was all she knew to do. Missing out on a proper education, Boudhsalinh read on a second-grade level.

Can you imagine immigrating to a foreign country, learning the language, and getting a job without a high school diploma? What would you do?

Our Victoria's Friends team fell in love with Boudhsalinh and her daughters, who were two and three years old, and immediately got to work on their behalf.

We found out Boudhsalinh was living in a bad area of Atlanta, not far from a cluster of strip clubs. Her home was a hotel room, where she left her precious daughters at night while she danced. Our team moved quickly to find suitable living quarters. Thankfully, a doctor and his wife from the church took them in.

It was a touchy and tricky time. Boudhsalinh remained in contact with the father of her children, Herieto, a local drug dealer who frequented the clubs.

We invited Boudhsalinh to our church's young adult singles gathering, and I'll never forget the time Herieto decided to make an appearance with a friend who called himself Crayon. To say that Crayon was a colorful character would be an understatement. The man was a pimp who hung out with the local drug dealers and strippers.

It was funny—and most likely a god-thing—that they arrived a little late and had to sit in the front row. I watched them squirm while the evening's presenter gave an uplifting, spiritual message.

Those open seats were also right next to one of the introverts and shiest of the ladies on our outreach team. (I will not embarrass this good friend of mine by naming her.) Herieto and Crayon's sitting next to her was another huge god-thing for my friend, as she was being stretched right in her own church. No need to go downtown for an outreach; the outreach came to her!

The music and message were on point for Herieto and Crayon. Those two were shocked by how good the program was. They clearly loved the message, which somehow got to them. We didn't see them again, but they left Boudhsalinh alone after that. I trust that God did His deep work in all parties present that night.

It takes a community; it truly does. Boudhsalinh received support from two residential programs run by nonprofits that provide a safe shelter for women and their children. The organizations further help adults acquire job skills and employment to become self-sufficient.

Several ministries in our community that rallied on the behalf of Boudhsalinh and her family deserve huge kudos.

Despite all efforts, Boudhsalinh could not so easily overcome her past. Words alone could never convey the brutal trauma she has suffered. I don't believe anyone survives that much trauma without Jesus! Therefore, although the seeds had been sown, Boudhsalinh wasn't ready. Until that time, she could not leave what was familiar.

She was dancing and stripping again when the unexpected happened: Marlene, the same person who'd answer Boudhsalinh's call on the first day and had become her precious mentor, passed away. Marilyn, another dedicated and determined member of Victoria's Friends, tracked down Boudhsalinh and invited her to the funeral. I believe this was the turning point. There's something about a funeral of a loved one, someone dear to us, that puts life into perspective. Soon after, Boudhsalinh left the strip club industry for good!

By the grace of God, her story has a happily-ever-after ending. Boudhsalinh plugged into Perimeter Church, joined the choir, and met a godly man who happens to be a doctor. The rest of this beautiful story (to date) is the happy marriage of two lovebirds. Boudhsalinh is enjoying her newly found faith and sharing it with the love of her life. God is a dream maker.

Boudhsalinh's journey with us and the other ministries spanned ten years and has continued in new ways. Her story—so rich with love, grace, and community—is a shining example of what happens when we all reach out and do our part. This is dispersion at work. Our light scattered throughout the community to help this one family.

No matter the mission, through our scattered efforts, as each one of us shines our light, we see how bright and far-reaching the effect can be. Embracing all that our Heavenly Father has for us allows us to turn back and scatter the light to others. The principle of dispersion perfectly applies to the way my Victoria's Friends outreach team operates.

Marilyn's determination to locate Boudhsalinh for Marlene's funeral adds another facet to this story, highlighting why we should not give up on others. We should keep shining brightly and scattering the light no matter how gloomy the situation appears.

While funeral plans for Marlene were underway, most of the team and the others who had helped Boudhsalinh were exhausted. Filled with their own grief, they probably were not thinking of her, but such an oversight would not have honored Marlene's memory. She had a been beautiful mentor with a fiery passion to serve the ladies of Victoria's Friends and set them free. Strongly connected to Boudhsalinh, Marlene would have insisted on finding and inviting her to the funeral. It was the right thing to do, but no one took the time or mustered the energy or will to do it except Marilyn.

Everything we do sets off an ongoing series of events and results. A great line from the movie *Gladiator*, when Maximus yells out to his troops, says it well: "What you do in life echoes in eternity." That is such a true statement.

When Boudhsalinh showed up for the funeral, all of eternity was set off. It was the defining moment that pulled her out of the darkness. Marilyn, in turn, will forever have a big jewel in her crown from making that one decision. I shudder, looking back at it and wondering what if Marilyn had not bothered or given up on an effort that was not easy.

Marilyn, by the way, was one of the attendees of the Callaway Gardens retreat (described in Chapter One) that set our hearts on fire and turned a group of ladies into powerhouses. She and her husband went on to adopt two very precious young girls. Marilyn tells the story in her words:

> It began in 2006, when my husband Tony and I were parenting three teenagers. In between many days of feeling overwhelmed, we went to a concert of Christian performing artist Steven Curtis Chapman. We heard his call to support adoption, which led to an invitation to Show Hope, the Chapmans' orphan

ministry. A mission trip to China with our family followed.

We all felt called to support the orphanage with our ministry of giving and contributed financially. Several times, people asked me if Tony and I were going to adopt. "No!" I answered emphatically, adding I didn't know what I was doing with the three I had.

No remained the answer until we visited a Children's Home in China that was full of older orphans. Sarah captured our hearts. I saw Tony on his knees, eyes tearing up, as he looked at her smiling face. She was standing next to three other little girls. His expression looked like the face of Jesus to me. His eyes sparkled with tears, shining with a calling from God. It was a holy moment. My face was more like a deer in headlights, dark with fear and overwhelming inadequacy.

After we returned home, it took me two months to get to a quiet time that ended my wrestling match. Jesus's words whispered to my heart, "Whatever you did for the least of these, you did for Me."

Revelation followed. Orphan Jesus doesn't need our money; He needs a forever family.

Steven Curtis Chapman's lyrics, "I saw the face of Jesus in a little orphan girl," closed the deal, leaving my face sparkling and shining in surrender to adopt.

What a rollercoaster those next two years were! Doors slammed shut on Sarah's adoption and on the twin sisters we tried next. We continued all the required paperwork; a literal foot-high pile accumulated. We did everything we could, praying with all our hearts, to no avail.

The Great Recession then hit our real estate business in 2008 like a tsunami, decimating the value of two, large construction projects, leaving us with unsupported, staggering debt. Trouble, fear, and despair attacked daily, interrupted by an incredible call that our twin girls had been released for our adoption! God's beautiful tapestry of miracles was revealed, offering evidence this was His will, even in this darkest valley. Could we really trust Him and find courage to obey?

By His grace, we did. We left for China in 2009 as a family of five and came back a family of seven with sparkling, bubbly, eleven-year-old twin girls, Maggie and Ginger, who could not speak English. Seven locust-devouring

business years continued, but He always provided, our new daughters saving us as much
as we saved them. They are now twenty-one-
year-old, bilingual, bicultural young ladies
who love Jesus.

Last year we celebrated their tenth year with
another China mission trip with Show Hope.
Our development business has been restored,
along with our ability to give to Kingdom
ministry.

Marilyn's testimony is a sparkling, shining one of
His incredible faithfulness and miraculous provision,
even for impossible callings.

We have this incredible connection to the Kingdom
of God. We see it so clearly when we serve others and
continue to do so, even when it is difficult. We also see
the light in our own trials and difficulties—if we do not
jump ship. We see the light of the Kingdom Connection
along with the scattered lights of others.

How do we disperse this Kingdom light?

- Stay with the situation: Be a Marilyn. Don't give
  up. A Dutch watchmaker, writer, and Christian,
  Corrie Ten Boom, who helped many Jews escape
  the Nazis, offered a fitting analogy: "When a
  train goes through a tunnel and it gets dark, you

don't throw away the ticket and jump off. You sit still and trust the engineer."

- Take initiative: When you see someone down or hurting or alone, reach out. Encourage a perfect stranger with a word of kindness or a smile. Use these moments to scatter your light.

- Pray: Ask God to work through us, our families, communities, and ministries.

- Show your joy: We need joy, and your joy can light up the skies. "Rejoice, Paul said, and again I say rejoice" (Philippians 4:4).

- Share and give: Love only grows by sharing. You can have more of yourself only by giving it away to others.

When our kids were little, my husband Jeff and I would take the family to his hometown of Decatur, Alabama, to visit his parents. Every year, we especially looked forward to the Alabama Jubilee Hot Air Balloon Classic. It was a spectacular festival. At least fifty hot air balloons in every color and theme you can imagine (cartoon characters, popular beverages, realtor advertisements—you name it) filled up a huge field. It was great fun with a live band and tons of good 'ole Southern food.

Of all the memories, the moments that remain etched in my mind happened just after sunset on the last night of the event. That's when the balloons were lit up, so they all glowed as they lifted off the ground and filled the darkened sky.

As I sit back and close my eyes, remembering how those beautiful balloons lit up the sky, I think of each of us. As we reach out to a dark and dying world to scatter our light, a spectacular lightshow sweeps across the sky. As we share our light with one another, beautiful souls, once dying, light up, one by one.

Let's light up the sky, ladies!

"While I am in the world, I am the Light of the world"

John 9:5

4

Kiss Me

"For above all else, the Christian life is a love affair of the heart."

– John Eldredge

*I*t was a night like any other. I crawled in bed, all cozy and cuddly, and drifted off. I am a deep sleeper. When I hit the pillow, I usually zonk out with no problem. Lulu, my Australian Shepherd, was curled in a ball at the end of my bed as usual. I fell asleep, only to wake up, feeling shaken and rattled to my core. As a cold chill went up and down my spine, I reached over to grab my husband. Sheer terror hit with a level of intensity that didn't seem possible for a dream. It was too real. However, I was having a vivid dream with a clear warning: I was in danger. I woke up knowing that if I did not turn back, I would die spiritually and, perhaps, physically as well.

Have you ever had a dream that told you something needed to change? This was one for me.

Several months before the dream, I'd been researching material for one of my book projects and ran across some Eastern practices that I'd followed during my time as a stripper. When I revisited them at first, the spiritual energy work seemed refreshing and fun, like a much-needed reprieve from a heavy season of spiritual warfare. Ministries go through different seasons, and some are taxing. If we're not careful, we can burn out. I believe, at that time, I was going through a bit of ministry burnout. Little did I know, I was like a unsuspecting frog in warm water that would gradually come to a boil.

Within the same period, as I was leaving my front yard with my three Aussies for our daily walk, I noticed my neighbor's evergreen had died. I was so sad because they had planted three, rather large and bushy trees that formed a wall, creating an attractive, fortress-like effect at the edge of our yards. Now, smack in the middle, the dead tree left a big, gaping hole.

The possibility that I was receiving a prophetic message didn't occur to me in that moment. Nonetheless, that's precisely what God had provided. My spiritual hedge of protection had a huge, gaping hole in it. I praise God that He loves me so much to have given me a wake-up call.

When I had that frightful dream, I'd been in the midst of bringing two guests to Atlanta for an event I was planning. Within the dream, a voice had clearly said, "If you bring them to Atlanta, you will be killed." After the threat, I felt as if I had been shot to death. That's when I woke up in the cold sweat. The impact was so startling that I canceled all plans the next day. For several days, I remained so unsettled that I didn't leave my home. Finally, I cried out to God, begging, "God, if You are still here for me, I need a sign. I need to know." A few days later, I received the answer, oddly enough, while I was giving my Aussies a grooming in the den of our home.

The room has high ceilings, allowing plenty of space for an ornately carved, eight-foot mirror that hangs over our fireplace mantle. The gold-leafed frame and beveled glass weigh about two hundred pounds; it's an impressive piece that reminds me of something that might have come from a castle. While attending to the dogs, I happened to look up. The mirror had caught a ray of sunlight, and a distinctive cross appeared. I naturally assumed the effect would be identical when the sun again hit the window from the same angle, but I've not seen it, not at all like the cross that formed on that afternoon.

I won't forget the feeling, the peace of God coming over me, as the cross appeared. I can best describe it as a peace that transcended all understanding. It was a sign from God with a calming effect, conveying everything would be alright. I knew He was with me. His presence wrapped around me and comforted me.

> "Stand at the crossroads and look;
>
> ask about the ancient paths,
>
> 'Which one is the good way?'
>
> Take it, and you will find rest for your souls"
> (Jeremiah 6:16).

I was definitely at a crossroads when I finally did venture outside my home for errands and ran into my dear friend Natalie. While talking, she invited me to join her for an inner-healing session with Pastor Summer and our friend Melissa. I accepted.

During the session, we went back through childhood abuse, and Jesus met with us in the most unique way. On previous occasions, my memories did not include Jesus. In that session, the first image I got in my mind's eye was of a man holding up and adoring an infant, representing a loving Father. My vision then shifted to a door, outlined by light, that invitingly ushered me into His presence. Simultaneously, a scripture verse impressed upon my spirit: *I am opening a door that no man can shut*" (Revelation 3:7).

The door opened to reveal the Lion of Judah. Strength and confidence entered me like never before. (That spirit has not left me.) The next day, my newsfeed on Facebook presented a picture of a little girl—she looked about three years old—with her legs tucked up to her chest as she nestled snugly into a lion's mane. I was meant to see myself as that girl. Another affirmation came in Pastor Johnson's sermon, which contained the message that the Baptism of the Holy Spirit is like unleashing a *lion* from your belly. When I got still before the Lord just to praise, I prayed, "Well, it looks like I'm back in alignment." In response, I heard the Holy Spirit say, "No, you are in a New Alignment! It's all new!"

Any person who has been in ministry for any length of time knows that different seasons emerge for different purposes. Some are birthing, growing, and expanding seasons. Some are intended as plateaus to stay right where you are for a while. The Word (Amplified Bible, or AMP) says the following in 2 Timothy 4:2:

> Preach the word [as an official messenger]; be ready when the time is right and *even* when it is not [keep your sense of urgency, whether the opportunity seems favorable or unfavorable, whether convenient or inconvenient, whether welcome or unwelcome]; correct [those who err in doctrine or behavior], warn [those who sin], exhort *and* encourage [those who are growing toward spiritual maturity], with inexhaustible patience and [faithful] teaching.

In other words, stay on top of your spiritual walk through every season. Don't falter or let your vision become blurry.

Several days after the sermon, as I was reading the Word, the following verse seared across the page (AMP):

> So, let's keep focused on that goal, those of us who want everything that God has for us. If any of you have something else in mind, something less than total commitment, God will clear your blurred vision. You'll see it yet! Now that we are on the right track, let's stay on it!

That was in December, and Victoria's Friends went on to have a highly successful month. God was clearly bringing it home for me in a loud and clear message. I share all of this to encourage us all to pay attention to our dreams and callings. We must stay the course.

As the New Year rolled in, our hearts were burning like never before. Thirty ladies were zealous about entering our twenty-one-day corporate fast, which we do every year. We were particularly excited about that year, our eleventh.

Even though I was super enthusiastic for our team, in the back of my head, I wondered if God's grace would not be there for me after I'd lost my spiritual fervor and focus for a bit in the prior year. I did not verbalize my concern, but it was definitely a thought that continued to come up.

Considering the unusually heightened level of anticipation for the fast, our church decided to host a nightly worship with glorious praise music over seven days. During the first three days, which are the most difficult days of consuming only fluids, the music especially eased the pain and got our focus on God. Truly, the fast is all about hearing from God. Overcome your flesh as you focus on the spirit!

Every service that week was meaningful, but no one will forget the seventh night. That's when Robin, my dear friend since high school, joined our worship. A true survivor who dearly loves the Lord, she shares her story:

> When I was young, a family member raped me. My mom had to take me to the doctor because of the physical wound it caused. However, I didn't tell anyone what happened until I became an adult. This was the beginning of how I saw myself and how I viewed love.
>
> As I got older, I realized I could get attention through sports. It was a great way to release the anger I had in me. In my senior year in high school, I got scholarship offers from several colleges, including the University of California and the University of Georgia, to play

basketball, but that wounded child was still there, full of fear, and I chose a smaller school in North Georgia.

I ended up pregnant right after practice started that year, and I had an abortion because, after all, I had this big basketball career pending. That was yet another deep wound that would haunt me for many years.

Excelling in basketball, I helped lead my team to Nationals, but in the last game of the season, I blew my knee out. That superstar identity was gone in an instant. All I had left was that wounded, unclean girl with ugly secrets.

I left college and was lost. I met someone and latched on to him. He seemed to really love me. I never knew, though, if he was going to come home and love me or verbally abuse me. We drank a lot. He was also a drug dealer. I used and abused drugs, but I didn't really like the drugs he was doing. I left him for another drug dealer, and his drug, meth, hooked me. It became my drug of choice.

We were wild and crazy on meth. Spiritually insane, I can remember standing in our bedroom, high on meth, arguing about something silly, I'm sure, when he grabbed my throat and choked me. I heard a pop. It doesn't take much pressure to the throat to actually kill someone. I remember not resisting. I remember not caring. The drugs numbed me out. The pain of my mistakes and things done to me had to be buried, and the meth was just the substance to do it.

A few years passed. I had gotten away from another toxic relationship and attempted to get off drugs, but I found someone to use with. I can remember looking in the mirror one day in pure hatred. I said, "I hate you! You are ugly!"

I then said, "God, if you can even hear me, You said that You would never leave me or forsake me. Help me!" I imagined all the angels in heaven cheering, "Finally, she has surrendered!"

Looking back, I believe that's when a heavy battle began to get me to the amazing, inner-healing ministry I found in North Georgia.

Today, Robin is on fire for the Lord with a deep, spiritual zeal. Her boyfriend permanently damaged her vocal cords when they were arguing, high on meth. Consequently, she lost her normal voice. Unable to speak in the middle range, she could only yell or whisper.

Excited that Robin had shown up on that seventh night of worship, I sensed electricity in the air from the moment the music started. (Have you ever had a heightened experience like that?) We all got quiet for our pastor to speak, and in that moment, a miracle occurred: Robin actually spoke five words in her normal voice. We all clearly heard her. Five words beautifully rolled out of her mouth. It was a supernatural sign from God. She hasn't been able to do it again, so we're all eagerly awaiting the next time and praying she regains the ability permanently.

God did not stop with Robin's voice. After praying for financial provision, I went on to get a special donation in the mail for Victoria's Friends. Next, unexpected jewelry—a beautiful cross and pearls on a gold necklace—arrived from a dear friend. The list went on and on. Our entire group was loved upon in a big way as prayer requests and blessings came in, one by one. The twenty-one days were loaded with blessing upon blessing for our team. Yes, we struggled through the fast, but God's thumbprint of love was evident. As we stayed the course with fasting and prayer, our group of thirty ladies bonded deeply.

One morning, when visiting our online fasting page, I saw that one of the ladies had posted a photo of a rainbow that had appeared with the sunrise. Driving to work, she'd spotted it right over her place of employment. Later, a few others posted rainbow photos, too.

The images made me pause, look up, and say, "God, You did all that! I know You did! Thank You, Father." I truly know it's not about us; it's all about the Father's love for us. It runs so deep and so wide.

Psalm 103:12 says: *"As far as the east is from the west, so far has he removed our transgressions from us."* All we have to do is look to Him with our palms open and say, "Here I am, Father. Forgive me and lead me." He will. Not only that, He will love our socks off! As we come home to God, He loves. He does not strike us down.

Besides getting docked (or temporarily pulled into a safe harbor) for straying off course, I received an extra measure of love on a cold, wintery night in February.

That evening, I picked up Louise, one of our precious Victoria's Friends ladies, and her two-year-old daughter for a worship service. Louise had her baby at the young age of seventeen, so at nineteen, she was still a baby with a baby. Having instantly fallen in love with those two, whom I consider my spiritual daughter and grandbaby, I proudly walked into church with the toddler on my hip. (I've adopted many spiritual children, as they have my heartstrings, and always say that it's amazing to receive a blessing as we minister to others.)

With no idea that we were about to tap into a new revelation of Jesus's intimacy that night, Louse and I both attentively listened to Pastor Johnson's sermon, entitled, "Kiss Me." He explained that prayer was never meant to be boring. He described the prayer as the place where Heaven touches the human heart, where God makes Himself vulnerable to us. Prayer, he said, is the place where God listens and moves on behalf of His beloved. As I have reflected throughout this book, prayer is one of the most powerful ways we can connect with God. It is the definition of intimacy with our Creator.

Why, then, is there such a giant void in prayer?

So many times, when we pray, if we are honest, we are praying to get our own way—not to be close to God, but to get things. Prayer should be an outpouring so we can be close to the heart of God and hear, connect, and commune with Him. We are sons and daughters of the living God. We need time with our Daddy Abba. Yet, so many people forfeit their time with busyness, trying to take matters into their own hands. All the while, God would gladly relieve us of our burdens if we would only turn to Him in prayer.

Our sincere prayers are not merely words blowing in the wind; they are a true heart-to-heart outpouring with our Heavenly Father. Our prayers are a huge aspect of our relationship with God. This is what we were made for. Relationship with God is our best life now.

Pastor Johnson went on to say that somebody was going to leave that night and go back into the arms of sex, pills, porn, and "your job" in an attempt "to find things that will make you whole." He went on to say that God Himself is the only One Who can make us whole.

Getting whole, he added, is not just about going to church; it's about communing with the Living God.

We must seek Him with our whole heart; otherwise, we will always choose the lesser ground: idols, addictions, busyness, or whatever it might be. Only the love affair with God will fill this void.

In all of our scrolling and our clicking and our swiping and our texting and our sexting, what we are chasing after is intimacy. Intimacy with God is the only thing that will touch the empty places of the heart. We are looking to be loved and known and appreciated and valued. A yearning for intimacy exists in the deepest places of who we are. If we are not finding that with God, in prayer, we will look for it somewhere else.

Louise and I were glued to Pastor Johnson's beautiful message, which continued with the "Song of Solomon," a biblical love story. Written between a husband and wife, the collection of love poems is also a beautiful shadow of our relationship with God and God's relationship with us.

"Let him kiss me with the kisses of his mouth.
For your love is better than wine"
Song of Solomon 1:2

The deepest cry inside the human soul is *kiss me*. We are crying out for love and intimacy and to be valued.

Kiss me is behind every needy heart. We want so desperately to feel loved.

When we do not meet *kiss me* in God, we go looking for it in other places. *Kiss me* becomes what we hope to find at the bottom of a bottle and in the bedroom. When we go to such places to be kissed, we find it is and will always be an empty imitation of intimacy. We're emptier than when we started because it leaves us with guilt, shame, and regret.

Kiss me was why I grabbed at my old roots in Eastern religion. I was searching in the wrong places. As the thought of that seared through my mind, I prayed, *Jesus, kiss me! I'll never leave you again. Fill those empty places in me, Father.* And He has. He truly has.

Let's make a habit going to God and saying, *Kiss me, and kiss me again, for your love is sweeter than wine.*

That evening was Louise's first time visiting our church, and what a first sermon for her to hear! While I don't know exactly what Louise was thinking, she accepted Christ that night. I know the angels in heaven were rejoicing. A deep revelation of the love Jesus has for us—and just how intimate that love is—pierced our hearts. The love was so deep that Louise and I both dropped to our knees. Louise met Jesus for the first time, and I fell more deeply in love with Him.

The next week, I was scrolling through my newsfeed on Facebook, when an image entitled, "The Hem of His Garment," took my breath away. A rare type of

Aurora Borealis (this one was spotted in Finland), the lights resemble the folds of a white curtain or, as many have observed, the hem of Jesus's garment. Taking a deep breath, I remembered Louise and me on our feet at the Hem of His Garment and thought of how our spirits must have lit up the winter sky!

As we bow down and touch the hem of His garment, our spirits truly light up as miraculously as the northern lights. Mighty things happen as we reach out in intimacy to our King.

How to shine our brightest:

- Tend to our hearts. Paying attention and listening to our dreams could very well save our lives. Sometimes God has to scream at us through our dreams.
- Empower ourselves by uniting with likeminded believers for fasting and prayer.
- Reach out to the lost for the double blessing of going further in our own walk.

"Arise, shine, for your light has come, and the glory of the Lord rises upon you"

Isaiah 60:1

5

Rough, Unpolished Diamonds

"One thing I do, forgetting what lies behind and straining forward to what lies ahead, I press on toward the goal for the prize of the upward call of God in Christ Jesus"

Philippians 3: 13-14

No matter who we are or where we are, we are all called to move forward.

It was the heat of a hot summer day in July when the hotline rang. "This is Victoria's Friends," our staff member answered. "Can I help you?"

"Yes, my girlfriend has been raped," answered the man. "She received a basket of love from your team six months ago, and I'm calling for help. She has very little family support."

Raised in a broken home by a mother who had multiple husbands, Brandi had a terrible start in life. She and her sister lived in poverty and were utterly neglected. Brandi's desperation led her to choose the sex industry to make ends meet. One night, having finished her late-night dance shift, she drove home to her apartment. While climbing the stairs to her unit, she heard someone and saw a man when she glanced over her shoulder. She was able to get the door open but frantically left the keys in the lock. Her attacker came in and beat and raped her—the worst nightmare imaginable.

Everything fell apart in the midst of this horrible event. After Brandi's boyfriend called our Victoria's Friends' hotline, we responded by counseling her and loving up on her in a big way. She quickly became my adopted daughter. A beautiful blonde with a tender spirit, she is lovely inside and out.

Brandi bonded with me, but as we first shared an irresistible love with her, the emotion did not register. She had good reason to be fearful, yet I knew God wanted to break into her heart and allow her to feel the love. We didn't give up. The days went by, and we continued to pour our love on Brandi. That love gave our courageous rock star strength to face her rapist in court.

I'll never forget the day she called and said she got it. She felt the love in a big way. We talked for hours and hours over the telephone. Brandi had accepted Jesus Christ as her Lord and Savior. She described the sensation of looking up and seeing everything in a different light. Colors were deeper and richer. She'd found the flow of God's love. Not long after that, Brandi also fell in love with an amazing guy. Her heart just opened up to let love in. Everything around her shifted.

Her life now is completely different. Brandi and her husband have two beautiful daughters, and she's living a wonderful lifestyle.

Impressing me the most was Brandi's willingness to do the hard work of delving into her wounds from childhood and the rape. For facing her rapist in court, she's one of the most courageous young ladies I know. Brandi had to revisit her wounds to get to the other side, but she did not go there alone. Jesus was with her on this healing journey. Consequently, as Brandi faced the pain and evil done to her, she could forgive the person and move on with her life.

Forgiveness is a key part of moving forward in our relationship with God and others. Forgiveness allows us to heal in the deep areas of real pain and real evil.

Some of the women associated with Victoria's Friends and I had the opportunity to offer a spiritual track through one of our church partners that entails an inner-healing course called Forward. After four classes, it concludes with an experience weekend. Designed by the staff at church, it delivers one of the deepest spiritual feedings I've ever experienced.

One of the sessions presents a powerful statement: Identity is our life filter. In other words, you can't know *who* you are until you know *whose* you are. Besides knowing, you must be willing, like Brandi, to address the wounds from childhood. A major area we deal with is the mother/father wound.

As defined by the course, mother/father wounds are "emotional wounds that were caused by the physical/emotional absence of the father/mother during the formative, developmental period of one's life." They result because a parent's methods of parenting were inadequate or overbearing. Therefore, such wounds materialize from a parent's action or inaction. For example, we all have a father, but, surprisingly, few of us have been fathered.

Our parents have such authority over us that something they do can stick with us for our whole lives and become impossible to shake outside of the power of Jesus Christ.

Dr. Frances MacNutt, a Roman Catholic priest who authored numerous books on healing, offered the following observation:

> When we were little, our parents took on something of the authority of God, and we absorbed their judgements were true. Even when children rebel against false parental

judgements (like, "you're stupid and will never amount to anything"), something deep down in the child believes it. These negative judgements—curses, really—may slice into the child like a knife and remain for a lifetime until Jesus frees him and replaces the lie with a true estimate of who he truly is. These distortions can destroy the child's self-esteem. (It is significant that shame, a feeling of basic worthlessness, is now seen as the root of all kinds of addiction.) This "hole in the soul" usually results from the child's belief that he has been rejected by the parents.

Are you struggling with this hole in your soul?

A vivid example of this message presented itself in the thick anointing that occurred when Pastor Israel from my church was sharing a childhood memory during the experience weekend. While he was learning to ride his bike, his father had a fit of rage. As young Israel kept falling, his father violently grabbed the bike and slammed it down.

As we listened and soaked in the spiritual feeding, God's presence permeated the air. Memories from my childhood then began to form in my mind's eye. I tried desperately to push them away. I struggled and asked myself, *Why?* The answer came: facing memories in this safe place was the reason I'd signed up for the weekend.

Letting the memories surface felt as if God were squeezing a toothpaste tube and pushing all the paste to the top to scrape it off. I relaxed as images of my childhood began pouring in. I was in a safe place to remember. Hearing Pastor Israel describe his pain gave me permission to remember mine.

It was all martinis, cigarettes, and wild parties throughout my childhood in Memphis, Tennessee. My dad was in the airline industry. My parents were part of a fast crowd, and they threw big parties. The homes in our neighborhood backed up to one another, forming a big circle, and every family would pitch in to purchase a big pig for our barbecues. Placed on a spit with an apple in its mouth, the pig would turn over and over a huge firepit. In the meantime, my sister and I would entertain the crowds. We were little girls. Topless, we'd wear Hawaiian leis around our necks and short skirts. I loved the attention it drew.

I remember dancing to "Aquarius/Let the Sunshine In," a popular 1960s' song performed by The 5th Dimension, as it played over the sound system. We were applauded by all the pilots—my dad's friends and neighbors—and whomever else seemed to make their way to the party. Vague memories of those days had surfaced from time to time, but at the conference, I relaxed my mind so the memory fully materialized.

I was seven years old when, in the midst of dancing with my leis to the crowd's delight, a man suddenly grabbed my hand and led me inside. He was a pilot who lived down the street from my family. Loud music and smoke filled the house. There were always so many people at the parties coming and going that no one noticed us.

When he said, "Come here. I have something for you," I was still high from all the attention of the crowd and eager to please him. Without concern, I followed him into one of the back bedrooms. He locked the door. "Dance for me, privately," he said. So, I did. "Come and sit on my lap," he added. Being seven, I did not know how to say *no*. I sat on his lap while he fondled me and spoke all kinds of flattering words about how pretty I was.

It ended when someone banged on the door and shouted, "Is my purse in there?" The pilot then reached in his pocket and pulled out a twenty-dollar bill. He told me, "Don't tell anyone about our special time together, and I'll bring you more money. *Shh*," he then warned, putting his fingers to my lips to hush me. "Get in the closet, and I'll open the door when you can come out."

My memory recreated the fear upon having the door shutting, trapping me in the closet, and then hearing voices in the room. Just when I was going to cry, he opened the door and let me out. I went back outside to the party. At seven, I was happy to have a twenty-dollar bill.

By letting the memory surface during the conference, Jesus took it right off the top. I would not have been strong enough to face it at other times in my life. I'd experienced too much other childhood trauma to process.

Considering everything, I knew the incident had made a huge imprint on who I became as an adult. I mentioned in the first chapter that my sister died of cancer, and a year later I was raped. I then slipped into the dark world of stripping and prostitution—clearly, reliving that moment from childhood over and over.

Many times, until something is healed, looked at, and dealt with, we repeat it.

Being molested at seven is one of the issues, I believe, that kept me in the stripping industry for four-and-a-half years. Something about dancing for men topless and receiving money felt familiar. The ability to recognize which childhood memories have marked us is important. Whether resulting from a parent or other authority figure, even a neighbor, as in my case, those damaging moments impact our adult lives and need to be healed.

So much of my behavior was about getting men to notice me. It didn't help that my father was busy with his career. I found myself always craving male attention, especially from men who were older than I. *Daddy, look at me. Tell me I'm special.*

The world is a dangerous place to enter as a young adult with a hole in your soul. I remained performance driven, seeking to be told I was special throughout much of my early adult years. I was in my late twenties when I accepted Christ and began the healing process. However, the healing journey unfolds in layers and takes many years.

We must deal with the holes in our souls to embrace our true identities. When I was in high school, I would never have said, "When I grow up, I want to be a stripper and prostitute." No one ever says that. Nevertheless, when you are walking around with a gaping hole in your soul, you will grab what's familiar.

When I let myself fully remember the incident that had tried to surface many other times, I felt a huge weight come off my spirit and soul. I cried tears of joy because I was truly free. I also embraced my new identity. I am an heir of the Kingdom of God.

> *"The Spirit Himself bears witness with our spirit that we are children of God, and if children then heirs"*
> **Romans 8: 16-17 NKJV**

No longer am I taking my clothes off, performing and dancing, looking for someone to tell me I'm special. I get it. I'm royalty!

The weekend also included an exercise of being still so we each could hear what God said about us. As I got very still, I saw the word *cherish* in my mind's eye. Webster's Dictionary defines cherish as follows:

> To treat with tenderness and affection, to nurture with care, to protect and aid. To hold dear and embrace with interest, to indulge, to encourage, to foster, to promote. One last definition, to properly hide and care for with affection.

Psalm 17:14 further says, "*you still the hunger of those whom you cherish.*"

What a beautiful scripture verse for me! No longer did I crave or hunger for the wrong attention of men. That hunger was hushed when I knew I was cherished and adored by God. Everything I ever wanted from my earthly father, I realized, was just what I got from God.

A seven-year-old little girl should be cherished, adored, loved, and protected. Now, as a child of God, I see firsthand His love, care, and protection over me. It is a beautiful and confident place to hang out. It comes with a God-inspired confidence that I didn't know was possible in my early years.

To note, our parents cannot give us what they did not receive themselves. I have the highest respect for my father, who pulled out of his childhood poverty and made a beautiful living for himself and our family. Years later, he also accepted Christ as his Lord and Savior. Currently, my father is active in his church and teaches a Bible study. I sincerely love my parents, who did a great job raising us with what they had been given. As tragedy blew in, we each dealt with it in our own ways. Through God's love and grace, we each found our way to Him.

We are *all* children of God and heirs to the Kingdom.

Oh, and about Pastor Israel who started our weekend session: He eventually got on his bike and rode and rode and rode into the sunset like a superhero! We can all ride into the sunset as superheroes. If we face the giants of abuse, we come to know those situations do not create our true identity. They reflect only what was spoken over us or done to us by broken people just like us.

To shine and shine brightly:

- Forgive – Our response to an offense determines our future. We can either let it go through forgiveness or let it grow. We choose.

- Pray – Any offense is a serious matter to God. He does not take it lightly. We must pray for the people who offend us and then give it to God and let it go.

- Identify – You can't know *who* we are until you know *whose* we are. *I am a child of God.*

Galatians 3:26 says, "For you are all children of God through faith in Christ Jesus."

- Meditate – What does God say about us? We must each meditate and rejoice over His word about who we are. *I am cherished as a child of the King.* Meditating on such nuggets is empowering.

In his book, *The Power of Real,* prolific author Bill Yount, who spent many years in the prison ministry, wrote the following:

I sense the Lord saying, "I'm releasing My glory through rough, unpolished diamonds in the earth, even many who have been rejected from My own house. Many of these vessels, who seem more 'earthy' than others, will begin to shine even brighter as My glory pierces through their cracked and broken vessels. The defects in some earthen vessels will actually give way to more of My glory shining through them."

The most valuable, finely cut diamonds in the world can be seen only in museums, under lock and key, never to be touched by human hands. Diamonds in the rough, however, can turn up anywhere and be touched by anyone. We, therefore, need to be careful upon deciding what exists inside other people. After they meet Jesus, the largest and most brilliant diamonds might appear before our very eyes.

Are you a diamond in the rough?

Brandi and I were diamonds in the rough. If He would take the broken pieces from our stories so that we could now shine, He will take yours, too!

"But we have this treasure in earthen vessels, that the excellency of the power may be of God, and not of us"

2 Corinthians 4:7 KJV

6

Acres of Diamonds

*"The biggest challenge in life is being yourself in a
world trying to make you like everyone else."*

– Victoria Teague

A Baptist minister and lawyer, Russel Conwell was
best known as the founder and first president of
Temple University. Years ago, he relayed a story that he
heard from his Arab guide in 1869, when the two were
beside the banks of the Tigris River.

As the tale goes, Ali Hafed owned a large farm with
one camel and a single plow to work the land. Although
he labored to make a living, Ali felt blessed and content.
He had all he could possibly desire, including a wife and
children.

One day, however, an old priest visited. Ali enjoyed
being hospitable. In the evening, as the two sat by the

fireplace talking, the priest told Ali about diamonds that had been discovered in a faraway land. Conveying their value, the priest remarked that just a handful of the gems could purchase an entire country. With a full mine of diamonds, Ali would have enough wealth to place each of his children on thrones. Hearing about such grand possibilities, Ali suddenly felt poor. In fact, he stayed up all night thinking of what he didn't possess but could, if only he could find diamonds.

The next morning, Ali begged the priest to tell him where he could locate the valuable gems. The priest replied, "If you find a river between high mountains that runs through white sands, in those white sands, you will always find diamonds."

With that, Ali was determined to search for them. After selling his farm, he said goodbye to his wife and children, declaring to them that he'd return a wealthy man. They'd have everything they desired for life.

Indeed, he traveled through the Middle East. He further went to East Africa and Europe, but Ali never found a single diamond. Reaching Spain, Ali had no money left. Desperate, he decided to end his life. He stood by the shore, and as soon as a giant wave came crashing towards him, he jumped in the raging waters. No one ever saw Ali again.

The man who bought Ali's property met a different fate. On an ordinary day, he took his camel (probably the same one that Ali once owned) to the stream for water. While the animal drank, the farmer happened to notice a glimmer of light in the stream. Curious about the source, he put his hand in the water and pulled out a dark stone. As he held it in the sun, the stone emitted a rainbow of light. Admiring the effect, the farmer kept the stone and placed it on his fireplace mantel back home. He thought nothing more of the decoration he'd found until the next day.

The same old priest who had visited Ali stopped by to visit the farmer. Casually chatting with the man while sitting beside the fireplace, the priest abruptly stopped talking. Seeing the black stone on the mantel, the priest exclaimed, "That's a diamond!"

The farmer was skeptical. "It's just a stone," he replied.

The priest, nonetheless, insisted it was a diamond and asked where the farmer had found it. The farmer led the priest to the stream. Together, they ran their fingers through the white, sandy bottom, and more diamonds than they could count appeared. Most were larger and shinier than the original one.

By selling his farm, Ali Hafed had led this man to discover Golconda, the most magnificent diamond mine in history. The mine would yield diamonds used in the crown jewels of the world's royalty, including those of England's Queen Mother. Ali Hafed had given up everything in search of what he desired yet already had. If he'd only remained home and continued to dig in his own fields, Ali would have found acres of diamonds.

Let's consider what we are searching to find or become.

We may feel stretched, inadequate, exhausted, or unqualified. We may feel that nothing God has promised is coming to pass in the place God has us. We resolve nothing by continuing to run off to the next thing. I meet so many women who are trying to be someone they are not and do what everyone else is doing.

I am reminded of Megan, a special young lady who was in my life for a season.

On the worst day of her life, her leg was amputated. What do you say, or how do you respond when your brave warrior has lost her leg to cancer? Only a very precious eighteen years old, she was young yet the bravest and most courageous of survivors.

As my daughter Hannah and I drove to the hospital, my thoughts spanned back to our ladies' group and Megan, the most physically striking among them. Some people are pretty; some are cute and adorable. Megan's in the category of knock-out gorgeous. Our group, however, was not focused on superficial matters. In fact, one of our first exercises together was to look up each one's name for the meaning.

We found that the name Megan is Anglo-Saxon in origin and means strong and capable. The name is also derived from Margaret, which traces to the ancient

Greek word for pearl. Also, the Celtic-Irish spelling comes from the ancient clan of Megan and in that context means brave warrior. Megan is a fitting name for someone strong and valuable. Although we didn't know it upon first gaining those insights, God knew. He knew what was ahead for her. In time, we, too, would learn and realize that our precious Megan was the bravest warrior of us all.

In contrast, I was only a visitor in the hospital, not the patient, but where was my bravery? Have you ever had golf balls in your throat? I sure did. I could feel them growing larger and larger as Hannah and I made our way from the hospital's parking lot to Megan's room.

What would we say to someone so precious who had her leg amputated the day before? I swallowed hard and cleared my throat. We didn't have to say anything. We just had to go and be there. Megan had other visitors besides Hannah and me, so we all shared and laughed— the best and only medicine we could offer.

When it was time to leave, I went to Megan's bedside and gave her the best bear hug I knew how to give. "Megan," I said, "my brave warrior, what can I do for you? How can I help?"

She looked me straight in the eye and said, "Ms. Victoria, just be you." Those words seared across my heart and broke me. **JUST BE YOU!**

Ladies, please take Megan's advice:

Just be you!

Remember, acres of diamonds are within you to sparkle and shine!

7

Don't Let Anything Dull Your Sparkle

*"But in your hearts revere Christ as Lord.
Always be prepared to give an answer to
everyone who asks you to give the reason
for the hope that you have. But do this
with gentleness and respect"*

1 Peter 3:15

While I was writing this chapter, the world was changing drastically. The coronavirus disease 2019 (COVID-19) became a pandemic. As of this writing, it hangs like a plague over the land. Thousands of cases have been documented as countries worldwide wonder if, how, and when we can return to our normal lives. What do we do? We cling to our faith, take a deep breath, and do the best we can to get through each day.

Doing our best to continue with normal routines, such as walking the dogs daily, my family and I have joined large numbers of folks in our neighborhood who are spending time outside. To prevent the spread of the virus, schools have been closed and businesses are ordering employees to work from home. Restaurants are closing their doors or remaining open only for take-out. The grocery stores are emptying their shelves just as quickly as they can restock because people are panicking that they soon won't be able to buy food.

My children are in college, and the reality that they'll complete their academic year through online classes has kicked in. To ease the disappointment, I invited my daughter and some of her friends to come over for a scenic hike around Lake Lanier, which is nearby. The view by the dam is especially beautiful. We had such a great time on the most crystal-clear, sunshiny spring day that we almost forgot about COVID-19. For a brief time, we were happily in the moment, hiking and enjoying nature, admiring a falcon as it flew overhead.

As we walked back to the house, I thought, *God is good. I am so grateful for my family, friends, and life.*

Later, while saying goodbye to Hannah and her friends, I had my three Australian Shepherds on their leashes, getting ready to walk. We were standing around Hannah's car, when my neighbor charged at me. In one swift move, he was right on top of us. With that, he let it rip, using colorful adjectives about my dogs and me, all in front of the young ladies. It was truly his worst moment to curse a woman and her dogs in front of her daughter and daughter's friends. The man was acting out terribly.

It happened so quickly that I sat back and just let him rip into me, up and down. What else could I do? He finished by concluding that he and his wife would be moving from the neighborhood because of me and my Aussies. As he walked off, all I could think to say was, "I hardly think that's the reason you will be moving."

My Aussies are my babies, and I've never had a single complaint about them from any neighbor. In fact, everyone loves them; they are fun-loving sweethearts. Also, I work and write quietly from home. While working, I've always left my back door open for the dogs to come and go in and out as they pleased. We have a fenced-in backyard, so they can't run off, but they will bark. Granted, if I happen to be on a hotline call, it might be a few minutes before I can break away to quiet them, but I don't let them bark nonstop.

The episode was upsetting to us all, but I decided to walk my dogs anyway, despite my neighbor's outburst. Still, I was burning mad, mentally spouting a few colorful adjectives of my own, trying to put everything into perspective. As I cooled off, I came upon an area of sidewalk where kids were having fun earlier. A child had written in pink chalk, "Don't let anything dull your sparkle." That message was straight from God, just as

I was finishing up *Sparkle and Shine*. Don't we love it when we know it's no coincidence!

Thank you, God! I know you've got this!

I was able to pray it off and put myself in his shoes. I even chuckled the rest of the way home. For perspective on the matter, while I'd been having all my feel-good moments on the hike, just the opposite was happening in the house next to ours. My neighbor had lost his job three months earlier, before the COVID-19 mayhem. All that time, he had been quarantined in a different way while at home, trying to find employment.

We have to realize that we're going to enter tense times in life. The way we respond can either put the fire out or make the flames rage out of control because we've essentially poured gasoline on it. Which will we choose?

On the day after that verbal assault, a job lead came in from someone with whom I had talked earlier about my neighbor's situation. I passed the information to his wife through a message that said, "I know it's rough right now, and we are praying for you guys. Let us know how we can help."

In this season, we must offer grace and deep love for a lost and hurting world. I'm carrying on with my Aussies and releasing love to my neighbors. The only reason I was able to push through that dark moment and others so quickly is because I have a spiritual connection to Jesus and a flow of His love. If our connection is not with Christ and His love, I've got big news: The world will not give it to us. The world is a scary place right now not to have Jesus Christ as our covering.

The world will try its best to knock us out of that flow. We only need to get still, pray, and hit the reset button. We must know that what we send out bounces back like a boomerang. I want love and blessings to bounce back to me.

I'm not perfect! Not any of us is. That's why, when we mess up, we ask God to forgive us, and we ask others to forgive us, if necessary, and move on in that flow of love.

As the world continued to shut down and the strip clubs all closed, Victoria's Friends immediately started a food pantry to serve single moms and other women who were not prepared. We further kept our hotline open.

During the crises, I received a call from Jenna, a dancer with an eighteen-month-old and no money. I prayed, and the Holy Spirit said to take her food and gift cards. While urging caution during a virus outbreak or in any type of intervention that posed risks, I would tell anyone to pray. God will show us what to do each time.

Sitting with Jenna at an outdoor park, I could tell she was frightened, so I asked if she had time to hear Pastor Jentezen Franklin's message. I could access it on my phone. With regular church services temporarily on hold, along with all other group gatherings suspended, I had been listening to Pastor Franklin online. He had a special service as part of the National Day of Prayer, and Jenna agreed to listen to it with me.

I took many mental notes from his service.

Pastor Franklin began by asserting that the building and the seats are not the church; the people are the church. With that, his other important cry was to choose faith over fear. When the world seems to be out of control, we need to know that God is certainly in control. During times that challenge us, such as when we have a pandemic underway, we need to come together, seek the face of God, and love and help one another.

He shared a story from Numbers 16 in the Old Testament about a plague that had killed thousands. The Lord spoke to Aaron, saying to burn incense in a censer. The particular type of burner hung from chains and, therefore, could swing back and forth. As clouds of smoke rose from the censer, Aaron was to go out to the plague-ridden land, where people were dying as easily as stalks of wheat being chopped for harvest, and to swing it back and forth, allowing incense to fill the air. Aaron did as he was told, and in the midst of his spreading incense among the living and the dead, the plague stopped.

The censer represents prayers and praise. As the Bible says, prayer and praise are like incense, going up to the Lord in the heavenlies.

Pastor Franklin went on to say that we are living longer and in healthier conditions than any other generation, so we should not make "much ado about nothing" (think and act as if circumstances are worse than they are) when our life is always in the Lord's hands. Instead, choose faith over fear. Don't let the "fear flu" get you. Get vaccinated with faith. Put the blood of the Lamb of Jesus Christ on your doorpost and watch death pass over your household. He commissioned us to read Psalm 91 over our families and feed our faith. Face the problem but focus on faith.

His message continued by acknowledging that so many of us were stuck in the middle of the valley of decision. We had to decide. Would we trust God in the midst of this trial? God says to trust Me, even though you are afraid. Faith first. Face it and fight it, and God says, *I'll do something about it.* God delights in courageous people. Jesus says, *I'll take care of you.* Declaring that we were in the middle of a divine shutdown in our nation, Pastor Franklin added, "When you are down to nothing, God's up to something."

When she heard those words, huge tears streamed down Jenna's face. She was truly down to nothing as we sat together at the park. She'd anticipated all I had to offer was a few bags of groceries and gift cards, but Jenna was about to receive a far greater gift.

The service continued with 2 Chronicles 20 in which the Israelites cried out to God, "We don't know what to do but our eyes are upon you." Pastor Franklin said to look up. Our God is bigger than the shutdown, bigger than coronavirus, and bigger than the stock market. However, if we were to be healed, it must begin with us on our knees, praying and humbling ourselves before God.

Faith is dependency on God. We had to put our faith in the One Who has conquered it all. He will never leave or forsake us. God so loved the world that He gave His only begotten son. We needed to receive the peace, the forgiveness, and the healing comfort of Jesus. We needed to pray, *Lord Jesus, I give you my life, my family, my future. I believe what you did on the cross was your love manifested for me. I receive salvation, forgiveness, and cleansing by the blood of Jesus Christ.* As we ask forgiveness for our sins, we should know that we are forgiven as we choose faith over fear in the mighty name of Jesus.

Jenna sat on that park bench and sobbed as she accepted Jesus Christ as her Lord and Savior. The hardest part for me was keeping the Centers for Disease Control's recommended six feet of physical distance between us; I could not touch or hug Jenna. Instead, I put out my arms in an air hug to let her know how delighted I was, giving us both the chuckle that we needed.

In the midst of a coronavirus pandemic or some other crises, do we know Jesus? He is our answer and the way out of any hot mess.

I was delighted that I had not given into fear over getting those groceries and gift cards to Jenna. God knew she would become His daughter that day. I certainly did not, but I'm delighted I got to be a part of it!

As this chapter demonstrates, two powerful elements to dull our sparkle are toxic people and fear. However, we hold the power to shine in the brightest possible way by making the following choices:

- Responding with love to toxic people and situations
- Being a blessing in a hurting world and receiving a boomerang blessing. What we put out to the world comes back to us.
- Choosing faith over fear
- Focusing on the belief that Jesus is bigger than coronavirus or any other calamity

Pastor Franklin's National Day of Prayer service concluded with singer Kari Jobe's powerful song, "The Blessing." The lyrics (found on YouTube) are as follows:

The Blessing
The Lord bless You and keep You
Make His face shine upon You
And Be gracious to You
The Lord turn His face upon You
And give You peace

The Lord bless You and keep You
Make His face shine upon You
And Be gracious to You
The Lord turn His face upon You

And give You peace
Amen Amen Amen
Amen Amen Amen
(repeat from top)

May His favor be upon You
And a thousand generations
And Your family and Your children
And their children and their children

In the morning in the evening
In Your coming and Your going
In Your weeping and rejoicing
He is for You, He is for You
He is for You ...

Amen Amen Amen
Amen Amen Amen

May His favor be upon You
And a thousand generations
And Your family and Your children
And their children and their children

May His presence go before You and behind You
And beside You all around You
And within You He is with You
In the morning in the evening
In Your coming and Your going
In Your weeping and rejoicing
He is for You, He is for You
He is for You...

God's Treasure Hunt

A 12-Day Devotion

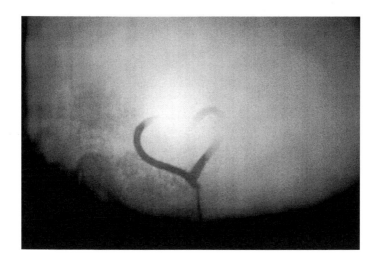

*Lord, how wonderful you are! You have stored up
so many good things for us, like a treasure chest
heaped up and spilling over with blessings—all
for those who honor and worship you! Everybody
knows what you can do for those who turn and
hide themselves in you.*

Psalm 31:19 TPT

God's Treasure Hunt

A 12-Day Devotion

We all have those moments where we've tapped into the amazing, irresistible love of God, those moments where He smothers us. Then the process begins. He peels back the layers of hurt and baggage we've carried for years and years. As we are truly purged and refined, we emerge as the Bride of Christ in all of her glory! Then the true journey begins. As we reach out to others and share this hope and treasure we have found, the true mystery of Christ begins.

May these twelve devotions help you, as you, too, discover the Mystery of Christ.

Introduction

My husband Jeff and I have always been into hiking; however, once we had children, our son and daughter slowed us down a bit. When Hannah was three, we could always count on her to pitch a fit on the trail. Sooner or later, Jeff would end up with her on his back. Hannah's dislike of hiking continued until we discovered geocaching.

Geocaching is a game in which players, known as geocachers, use GPS receivers to track down treasures that are hidden in containers, referred to as caches, by other players. While they are treasure hunting, geocachers also explore interesting locations. As one who has always loved a great treasure hunt, I am among thousands of people around the world who are hooked on geocaching.

A guiding principle of geocaching is "take something, leave something." To start the game, the first hider places a number of goodies in a container. As different people locate the cache, they exchange items that catch their eyes with treasures they've brought with them on the search.

Geocaching turned hiking into a family adventure that delighted our kids, my husband, and me. We went all over, looking for caches and collecting and leaving little gifts, including poems and fun trinkets.

Did you know that God has created a treasure hunt for all of us as we navigate our lives?

Among the jewels that He left for us to discover are true treasures that are found in hidden places in which only His children will have eyes to see.

How do we find them?

Just as my husband, kids, and I used a map for our geocaching, we have a guide to find His special gifts. We can begin with the map He gave us: The Word.

As we look at His word, we can each ask God to go on a treasure hunt with us. That's when we'll discover a life that is not only priceless to us now, but also promises an inheritance of eternal jewels. Anything we do for God's Kingdom is a treasure stored up in Heaven that can never be stolen—neither now nor in all eternity. We must remember that each of us is God's greatest treasure. Each one of us is a jewel that sparkles in the crown of our King. He wants His children to shine brightly for all to see.

Together, we can dig for some of those precious jewels by following the twelve-day devotion I've created. I've gleaned the nuggets from my treasure hunting in the Bible for the last thirty years as well as through my interactions with pastors, counselors, friends, the ladies of Victoria's Friends, and my family, all of whom are on the same treasure hunt.

Let's dig deeply. I promise, the most beautiful gems and jewels are waiting to be found.

"The kingdom of heaven is like treasure hidden in a field. When a man found it, he hid it again, and then in his joy went and sold all he had and bought that field"

Matthew 13:44

Tapping Into Love

And I pray that you, being rooted and established in love, **18** *may have power, together with all the Lord's holy people, to grasp how wide and long and high and deep is the love of Christ,* **19** *and to know this love that surpasses knowledge—that you may be filled to the measure of all the fullness of God.*

Eph 3: 17-19

*"Wherever your treasure is, there the
desires of your heart will also be"*

Luke 12:34

Since the beginning of time, humans have prized earth's sparkling treasures, and many have devoted their lives to searching for all kinds of hidden gems. Modern-day prospectors use advanced drilling and excavation technologies to retrieve mineral deposits. Nevertheless, people of all ages still enjoy the thrill of digging with their own two hands or simple tools until they unearth something special. That's why panning for gold remains a popular hobby or vacation adventure. Never knowing just what they'll find, young and old are drawn to prospecting.

All along, we are called to be spiritual prospectors. Will we get dirty? Yes! We'll likely end up with muddy hands and dusty faces. But, as Christians, we are called to persevere. In spite of the mud and dirt, we are called to dig just beneath the gross and dark places on earth. Once there, wearing the dirt of our efforts, we discover the greatest hidden treasures.

The most spectacular deposit of gold that the Lord helped me unearth is love. Finding His love was so huge that I couldn't get over it, around it, or underneath it. It was so big that I couldn't completely comprehend it. I can best describe my perception of God's love as a raging wildfire. It chases all of us, and, in the process, surpasses all knowledge and understanding.

His unconditional love is beginning to invade the earth in this hour. God's love is invading us all. Many people are experiencing it.

For some of us, it happens on those days when things are not that great, and we feel like we have blown it. For others of us, it occurs when all hell has broken loose, and we know we have blown it bigtime. In those moments, God sneaks up on us, outrunning us, to say, *I love you! I still love you. I don't love you because you are good or bad. I love you—period. You can't earn My love; you can only receive it. You can't fail enough to stop Me from loving you.*

When you have this revelation, you will love Him back with all your heart, mind, body, and strength. It will cause you to love others deeply with the love of Christ that transcends all understanding. When you taste of this love, you will drop all the foolish things you have been chasing after and wake up in love with Jesus.

When *the* love breaks through, you will be fully awake in Him for Kingdom purposes.

We each have a passion inside us to do something bigger than ourselves. God's plan for our lives has already been put into motion; however, we remain in a holding pattern until God alone is enough for us. Because God loves us, His ultimate plan for us will unfold when we seek Him with our whole heart. We go through a process as we grow closer and closer to Him.

Let the process begin.

Devotion, Day 1

Father, thank You for the love, this irresistible love. I am ready to follow You with my whole heart. Lead me, guide me, and direct me into Your perfect plan for my life. I don't want my life driven by anything but love for You. Help me to center my life on Your plan and purpose for me and not to worry about the expectations of others. As I dig into Your Word, I trust that Your plan for my life is unfolding. I keep my heart and my passion for You and You alone.

Reflections

"And now these three remain: faith, hope and love. But the greatest of these is love"

1 Corinthians 13:13

_____

_____

_____

_____

_____

_____

_____

_____

_____

_____

_____

_____

_____

_____

_____

_____

_____

_____

_____

The Purging Refining Process

*"The crucible for silver and the furnace
for gold, but the LORD tests
the heart"*

Proverbs 17:3

"We went through fire and flood. But in the end, you brought us into wealth and great abundance"

Psalm 66:12

As I have centered my plans on God and His plan for my life, I've noticed patterns and seasons that emerge in following Christ. It looks different for each of us, but a pattern exists. When we expect and look forward to them, just as we anticipate the seasons of the year, we gain an understanding of our spiritual walks and callings.

Here's an illustration:

From the beginning of time, fire and water have been two of man's most essential needs. We cannot live without either, but they both can cause great havoc. In 2019, Southern California experienced raging forest fires that destroyed hundreds of beautiful homes, cars, landscapes, and anything that got in the flames' way. As firefighters finally tamed and extinguished the burning, and as people began to clear pathways for construction and rebuild, they became aware of a new problem. A priceless watershed had been destroyed.

This watershed—connected to suburban lawns, parking lots, and city streets—served a strategic purpose. Water would seep down through the soil to aquifers, which are underground rivers. Flowing below the ground, the water could escape slowly to outlet points, such as springs, rivers, lakes, and oceans. With the watershed ruined, winter rains posed a problem of flooding. Thus, the same water that ended the chaotic fires suddenly became a dangerous threat to the land.

In looking at our trials, the psalmist put it this way:

"We went through fire and flood.
But in the end, you brought us into wealth
and great abundance"

Psalm 66:12

Wealth and abundance go hand in hand. They speak to an expansive place with healing and nourishment. God describes our trials, troubles, and afflictions as fire and water, pointing to devastation. But our jewel shows us the word *through.* We know, then, that He is always there to help us through and beyond the challenges.

Devotion, Day 2

Father, as I pass through trials, help me to remember that it is a passing through. Joy, victory, and comfort are awaiting me. I wait for You, knowing You are bringing me into wealth and great abundance.

> When you pass through the waters,
> I will be with you;
> and when you pass through the rivers,
> they will not sweep over you.
> When you walk through the fire,
> you will not be burned;
> the flames will not set you ablaze.

Isaiah 43:2

Reflections

*"Consider it pure joy, my brothers and sisters,[a]
whenever you face trials of many kinds, ³ because
you know that the testing of your faith produces
perseverance. ⁴ Let perseverance finish its work so
that you may be mature and complete,
not lacking anything."*

James 1:2-4

_____

_____

_____

_____

_____

_____

_____

_____

_____

_____

_____

_____

_____

_____

_____

_____

_____

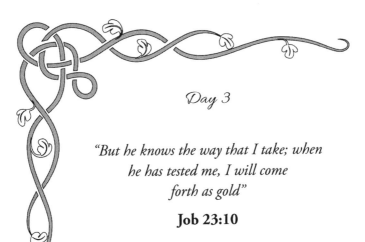

Day 3

*"But he knows the way that I take; when
he has tested me, I will come
forth as gold"*

Job 23:10

We all go through a refining and purging process in our spiritual journeys. As we come into deeper levels of spiritual understanding and grow closer to our heavenly Father, we are all tested.

Immediately after I accepted Christ as my Lord and Savior, I was kicked out on the streets. While I sat at a Waffle House, trying to figure out whom to call and where to go, I pulled out a little Gideon Bible from my purse and turned to the Book of Job. I read that he suffered with oozing boils that he scraped with broken pieces of pottery. Flashes of hot pain shot through his body. Fever parched his lips. His head throbbed. If that was not enough, Job's friends falsely accused him. In the midst of it all, he says, "I shall come forth as gold."

Job saw himself as gold in the furnace. David saw the children of God "as Silver is tried" (Psalm 66:10). Malachi links both metals together in explaining divine chastening. "And he shall sit as a refiner and purifier of silver and purge them as gold and silver" (Malachi 3:3). Why? "That they might offer unto the Lord an offering of righteousness."

We must remember, as we are stripped down and refined in the fires of a trial, God is producing something brand new in us. We must hold the position that we are going through it for Him to position us as silver and gold. It's hard to trust God's methods, but the pattern I've seen over and over again is threefold:

The Divine Method – Fire

The Divine Motive – Purge and Purify

The Divine Objective – Our Righteousness

There are many lessons to learn from this refining and purging process.

Devotion, Day 3

Father, help me to be just like Job in the midst of the trial, to claim, *I shall come forth as gold.* It is one thing to testify after I've come through the trial, but Job was still in the furnace when he claimed this. Father, strengthen me, and carry me, and let me see that You have me in the refiner's fire for a divine reason. I claim I shall come forth as gold.

Reflections

*"He will sit as a refiner and purifier of silver; he
will purify the Levites and refine them like gold
and silver. Then the Lord will have men who will
bring offerings in righteousness"*

Malachi 3:3

_____

_____

_____

_____

_____

_____

_____

_____

_____

_____

_____

_____

_____

_____

_____

_____

_____

_____

_____

"Humble yourselves, therefore, under the mighty hand of God so that at the proper time He may exalt you, casting all your anxieties on Him, because He cares for you"

1 Peter 5.6-7

After I birthed my ministry, I was so frustrated. It was a time of great testing. Many things were coming at me from all directions, and it was hard to decipher what was going on. Finally, in the midst of my frustration, I got still during my private devotion time. As I worshipped and praised God, I heard His gentle voice again. The Lord whispered in my ear, *Victoria, I am for you.* Again, I got still and heard, *Victoria, I am for you.*

In response, I prayed, "Lord, it does not feel like you are for me. I feel like the entire world is against me right now."

His gentle voice, however, continued: *Not only am I for you, I am crazy about you.*

I said, "What?" as tears rolled down my cheeks. "I fall so short."

God then said something incredibly strange: *I know you do, but you trust me. You continue to trust me while the storms are raging against you. You still trust me to do what you cannot do. That thrills me and that's what makes me crazy about you.*

Let's never doubt God's care, especially during the testing and trial and purging season. During this time, we might doubt God's love for us if we are not careful with our thoughts and actions. Nonetheless, we are God's most prized possessions, and He will allow nothing to harm us. All things pass through His mighty hands, and that thing that happened to you is His means of increasing the value of His precious property. This is accomplished by increasing our beauty and purity, although it does not feel that way at the time of testing. However, if we were worthless objects, we would never know the heat of the Refiner's fire or the touch of His skillful hand. Therefore, while feeling the heat of this fiery trial, we must thank God. In this proof of our preciousness to Him, we are assured that He cares for His own.

Devotion, Day 4

Father, it is difficult right now. As I am up under Your refining fire, speak to me. Assure me of Your caring and gentle touch. Show me Your goodness and that You love me. Show me that You are crazy about me. Lord, I trust You during this test.

Reflections

> *"What, then, shall we say in response to these*
> *things, If God is for us, who can be against us"*
>
> *Romans 8:31*

_____

_____

_____

_____

_____

_____

_____

_____

_____

_____

_____

_____

_____

_____

_____

_____

_____

_____

_____

_____

Day 5

*"Purify me with hyssop, and I shall be
clean; Wash me, and I shall be
whiter than snow"*

Psalm 51:7

In helping ladies escape the sex industry, Victoria's Friends will pay their rent and cover some of their bills during their job training to move forward in life. I was really frustrated with one of the ladies we had been supporting because she was never grateful. Her donors had been more than gracious, but she would text and text and ask for more and more. Finally, in frustration I reminded her of the agreement we had and said if this was not working for her, we did not have to continue.

After that, she completely changed her position. She finally got it and became more thankful in our future correspondence. As her entitlement issues began to roll off, she ended up being a delight to work with.

When she had been demonstrating an ungrateful attitude, I noticed that I wanted to do less for her and more for the ones who were gracious. One day, while I was in my prayer closet, the Lord showed me that I had been like this young lady in how I'd been thinking that a particular church should do more. Amazingly, I clearly realized that my lack of gratitude was affecting the support we received from that church. Ouch! I repented, and God immediately opened doors for me at that very church. They are currently a delight for me, and, I believe, I'm a delight for them as well.

Let's spend some time in reflection before the Lord today. What kind of dross (rubbish) in our life should we purge: arrogance, pride, love of praise, love of attention, self-will, stubbornness, an unteachable spirit, love of money, selfishness, entitlement issues, or an unforgiving spirit?

The list could go on and on with endless issues. What we refer to as *dross* really amounts to the deeds of the flesh. All of it grieves the Holy Spirit who dwells within us, so we must be refined and purged. This means we must pass through the fire, but there's some comfort here for us.

There is always a purpose with the Refiner. It is not to destroy His precious silver and gold, but to consume the dross and bring out the beauty and purity of the gold. Fire cannot destroy the gold; it only melts it. Oh, how we need to be melted before God. When the gold is melted, the dross floats to the top, and it's easy for the Refiner to skim it off.

How long has it been since any of us has been melted?

Devotion, Day 5

Father, cleanse me of all my dross. The flesh is weak, and the spirit is strong. Make my spirit even stronger. Search me and cleanse me that I might be as pure gold before You.

> *"Search me, God, and know my heart;*
> *test me and know my anxious thoughts.*
> *See if there is any offensive way in me,*
> *and lead me in the way everlasting"*

Psalm 139: 23, 24

Reflections

*"After your season of suffering, God in all His
grace will restore, confirm, strengthen
and restore you"*

1 Peter 5:10

_____

_____

_____

_____

_____

_____

_____

_____

_____

_____

_____

_____

_____

_____

_____

_____

_____

_____

Day 6

"But you are a chosen people, a royal priesthood, a holy nation, God's special possession, that you may declare the praises of him who called you out of darkness into his wonderful light"

1 Peter 2: 9

After we go through the purging-refining cycle, a new birth and a strong identity emerge. When the purging-refining cycle finally does its work, the effect is similar to squeezing a tube of toothpaste to the top and then scraping off what comes out. The dross comes up, and it's ugly, yet God takes it and removes it from our life. A lightness then enters, and we are able to hear and see more clearly where we are heading in Christ.

His purposes for our lives become clear.

I compare this season to the experience of going out to blaze a hiking trail after a storm. Branches and debris are scattered everywhere, and portions of the trail are wiped out. Two days later, however, we can go back and find that the park rangers have cleared the way. All of a sudden, we can see the path again, and our direction going forward makes sense.

We know whose we are and where we are headed. We know who we are in Christ.

Devotion, Day 6

Lord Jesus, I praise You and thank You for all of the benefits in the Kingdom because of You and Your great love for me.

Reflections

*"And when the Great Shepherd appears, you will
receive a crown of never-ending glory and honor"*

1 Peter 5:4 NLT

_____

_____

_____

_____

_____

_____

_____

_____

_____

_____

_____

_____

_____

_____

_____

_____

_____

_____

_____

_____

_____

_____

Day 7

*"You have made them to be a kingdom
and priests to our God; and they will
reign upon the earth"*

Revelation 5:10

*Y*our royal identity in Christ is secure.
The entire concept of royalty in Christ was
once so foreign to me because I had chosen
to live my life in such an opposite manner. I lived
eleven years as a vagabond from hotel to hotel
and from man to man. After I accepted Christ
and immersed myself in the Word, it amazed me
to find out that I am a daughter of the King!

I am a princess. I am royalty.

Carrying this in our spirit changes the way
we live, but how are we royalty? How could it be?
It seems too good to be true.

There are several ways in which we are royalty in Christ. First of all, we are royal by birth.
When we receive Jesus as our Lord and Savior,

we are spiritually born into the royal family of God. That makes us royal by birth.

Second, we are royal by marriage. As the bride of Christ, our Bridegroom is the King of kings and Lord of lords. As a bride to the King, we are royal by marriage.

Finally, we are royal because God destined us to be royal. His plan was to have a nation of royal priests. He called us to a divine and royal purpose … to rule and reign with Christ (2 Timothy 2:1).

Devotion, Day 7

Today, let's look at the ways that we are not living as royalty. Let's ask God to show us if we need to rise up higher in our thoughts and ways. Let's rejoice and thank God for our position in Him.

Reflections

*"But you are a chosen people, a royal priesthood,
a holy nation, God's special possession, that you
may declare the praises of him who called you out
of darkness into his wonderful light"*

1 Peter 2:9

_____

_____

_____

_____

_____

_____

_____

_____

_____

_____

_____

_____

_____

_____

_____

_____

_____

_____

_____

"See what great love the Father has lavished on us, that we should be called children of God! And that is what we are! The reason the world does not know us is that it did not know him"

1 John 3:1

od gave us a royal identity when we became a part of His family. We are destined to rule and reign with Christ.

We were created to feel safe, secure, confident, and bold; it's part of our spiritual DNA as daughters of the King. The key to living a secure life in Christ is knowing who we are in Him. Really receiving God's love for us, basing our worth and value on who God says we are, not what we do, is an essential part of it.

"But you are God's chosen treasure—Priests who are kings, a spiritual 'nation' set apart as God's devoted ones. He called you out of

darkness to experience his marvelous light, and now
he claims you as HIS very own. He did this so that
you would broadcast his glorious wonders through-
out the world. For at one time you were not God's
people, but now you are. At one time you knew
nothing of God's mercy, because you hadn't received
it yet, but now you are drenched with it"

1 Peter 2:9-10 TPT

When we have the foundation of who we are in Christ, then we can go and change the world!

A Spiritual Exercise: Find the Treasures

Let's pour over the following verses with the words *trea-sure* and *jewels*. As we absorb the meaning, we should remember that God's Word is our greatest treasure, and each of us are *jewels* in the crown of the King!

"I consider your prophecies to be my greatest
treasure, and I memorize them and write them
on my heart to keep me from committing sin's
treason against you"

Psalm 119:11 TPT

"Throughout the night I think of you, dear God;
I treasure your every word to me"

Psalm 119:55 TPT

*"Proud boasters make up lies about me because
I am passionate to follow all that you say. Their
hearts are dull and void of feelings, but I find my
true treasure in your truth"*

Psalm 119:70 TPT

*"Everything you speak to me is like a joyous
treasure, filling my life with gladness"*

Psalm 119:111 TPT

*"Truly, your message of truth means more to me
than a vault filled with the purest gold"*

Psalm 119:127 TPT

*"Look at the splendor of your skies, your creative
genius glowing in the heavens. When I gaze at
your moon and your stars, mounted like JEW-
ELS in their settings, I know you are the fascinat-
ing artist who fashioned it all"*

Psalm 8:3 TPT

*"Don't keep hoarding for yourselves earthly trea-
sures that can be stolen by thieves. Material wealth
eventually rusts, decays, and loses its value. 20
Instead, stockpile heavenly treasures for yourselves
that cannot be stolen and will never rust, decay,*

*or lose their value. 21 For your heart will always
pursue what you value as your treasure"*

Matthew 6:19-21 TPT

*"We are like common clay jars that carry this
glorious treasure within, so that the extraordinary
overflow of power will be seen as God's, not ours.
8 Though we experience every kind of pressure,
we're not crushed. At times we don't know what
to do, but quitting is not an option. 9 We are
persecuted by others, but God has not forsaken us.
We may be knocked down, but not out"*

2 Corinthians 4:7-9 TPT

*"But you are god's chosen treasure-Priests who
are kings, a spiritual "nation" set apart as
God's devoted ones. He called you out of darkness to experience his marvelous light, and now
he claims you as HIS very own. He did this so
that you would broadcast his glorious wonders
throughout the world. For at one time you were
not God's people, but now you are. At one time
you knew nothing of God's mercy, because you
hadn't received it yet, but now you are
drenched with it"*

1 Peter 2:9-10 TPT

"On that day the Lord their God will rescue his people,
just as a shepherd rescues his sheep.
They will sparkle in his land
like jewels in a crown"

Zechariah 9:16 NIV

"To everyone who is victorious I will let him feast
on the hidden manna and give him a shining
white stone. And written upon the white stone is
inscribed his new name, known only to the one
who receives it"

Revelation 2:17

"Again the word of the Lord came to me saying,
'Son of man, take up a lamentation over the king
of Tyre and say to him, 'Thus says the Lord God,
'You had the seal of perfection,
Full of wisdom and perfect in beauty.
'You were in Eden, the garden of God;
Every precious stone was your covering:
The ruby, the topaz and the diamond;
The beryl, the onyx and the jasper;
The lapis lazuli, the turquoise and the emerald;
And the gold, the workmanship of your
settings and sockets, Was in you.
On the day that you were created
They were prepared"

Ezekiel 28:11-13

"The material of the wall was jasper; and the city was pure gold, like clear glass. The foundation stones of the city wall were adorned with every kind of precious stone. The first foundation stone was jasper; the second, sapphire; the third, chalcedony; the fourth, emerald; the fifth, sardonyx; the sixth, sardius; the seventh, chrysolite; the eighth, beryl; the ninth, topaz; the tenth, chrysoprase; the eleventh, jacinth; the twelfth, amethyst.

And the twelve gates were twelve pearls; each one of the gates was a single pearl. And the street of the city was pure gold, like transparent glass"

Revelation 21:18-21

"I will rejoice greatly in the Lord,
My soul will exult in my God;
For He has clothed me with garments of salvation,
He has wrapped me with a robe of righteousness,
As a bridegroom decks himself with a garland,
And as a bride adorns herself with her jewels"

Isaiah 61:10

When we continue our treasure hunt in the Word, we'll find many more jewels in the treasure chest. God has written it all out in His love letter to us. The Word is there for us all to discover.

Devotion, Day 8

Lord Jesus, I know You approve of me and that is all that truly matters. If I live by man's approval, I will die by their rejection. Your love for me isn't based on what I do or how well I perform. I choose to be secure in Your love, knowing I am Yours and You are mine. When I struggle, pull me back and remind me of my identity. I pray I become stronger every day in my walk with You. In Jesus's name, Amen.

Reflections

*"Yet to all who did receive him, to those who
believed in his name, he gave the right to become
children of God"*

John 1:12

_____

_____

_____

_____

_____

_____

_____

_____

_____

_____

_____

_____

_____

_____

_____

_____

_____

_____

_____

_____

A Deeper Level of Mystery
of Christ

He replied, "The mystery of the kingdom of God has been given to you, but to those on the outside everything is expressed in parables."

Mark 4:11

"Set a guard over my mouth, Lord; keep watch over the door of my lips"

Psalm 141:3

As women, I am amazed how quickly we can flip back and forth between blessing and belittling, praising and putting down, cheering and critiquing—all in a matter of seconds. God has given us incredible power in our sphere of influence, and it begins with the words we speak.

Today I want to caution us to pay attention to the power of our words. We have a great opportunity to encourage and bless others or tear down and criticize them.

When we are having difficulty with our mouth, we must pray the Word. God's word carries the power of His Spirit. His word is medicine for our soul. It enables us to lead a life that is pleasing before His sight. The key is for each of us to do our part and allow God to do His.

He does not need our help, even though, sometimes, we think He does.

We must be intentional in overcoming idle talk and negativity. We must remember that it all starts in the mind. Where the mind goes, the man will follow. As we grow and mature in our walk with Christ, we will notice the negativity dying and the positivity rising. This is part of the process of becoming a conqueror and knowing who we truly are.

So, here's the question for us: How will we use the incredible gift of the words that God has given us today?

Devotion, Day 9

Lord Jesus, I pray that You will help me to develop sensitivity to the Spirit concerning all manner of conversation. I want to move in Your direction with a gentle nudge from You. Place a guard over my lips and let all words of idle talk cease. Allow the words of my mouth to be acceptable in Your sight. O, Lord, You are my Strength and my Redeemer. I thank You for guiding my conversation. In Jesus's name I pray, Amen.

Reflections

*"Let your conversation be always full of grace,
seasoned with salt, so that you may know how to
answer everyone"*

Col. 4:6

_____

_____

_____

_____

_____

_____

_____

_____

_____

_____

_____

_____

_____

_____

_____

_____

_____

_____

_____

_____

_____

"And whatsoever ye do, do it heartily, as to the Lord and not unto men. Knowing that of the Lord ye shall receive the reward of the inheritance: for ye serve the Lord Christ"

Colossians 3:23-24

*L*ord, I want to be close to You. I want to walk with You and know more of You. I need to feel Your Spirit within me. I need a word, a sign, just anything, Lord, let me know You are here with me.

How many of us find ourselves praying something like that? We say a heartfelt prayer then get busy. We don't sit at the master's feet to listen. Instead, we pray and then hurriedly get up and wonder why it didn't happen yet.

Guilty, we all are. God is not a genie in a bottle. We don't have to rub the vase, wait for Him to come, and grant us a wish. His wish is for us to *know who we are in Him* so that we can become the joint heir He intended for us to be. *Everything that is His* is ours. In our fleshly mind, we cannot begin to comprehend that. We analyze, question, debate, and confuse our own selves. All the while, He is just calling us to come as we are, to learn and grow in Him.

I use the time when I'm out for a morning walk to mediate, pray, and seek. On one of those occasions, as I was talking to the Lord, I began to tell Him that I wanted to go up higher. I wanted to grow in Him and to win souls for His kingdom. I wanted Him to help me to *be* more, *love* more, *give* more, and *grow* more.

My thirty-minute walk was coming to an end, so I glanced at my watch, counting down the seconds to be finished. I was tired. The hill I was climbing had been steep, and my thighs were burning. I was gasping for air. I pushed *end* on my watch and thought, *Yes, I am done!* That's when I heard that still, small voice of Jesus. He whispered to me, lovingly yet sternly:

You want more? You want to grow? You want to be a soul winner? Then go the extra mile. You meet your goals, but you never push past them for more.

He was speaking to my spirituality. He wasn't telling me to go exercise more, but to press in more to Him, to show Him that I would put in the work.

I was willing to sacrifice a few meals with fasting and prayer; to hit my prayer closet seeking His face and not His hand; to grow more intimate in my relationship with my King. I have to be honest, however, and confess that I was not operating with much conviction. No, I had neither been sinful nor lazy, but I had been doing only what I needed to do and nothing more.

I decided to keep walking and praying, and go the extra mile. Physically and spiritually, I obeyed.

Everything was good right where I was, yet I suddenly remembered that I am not called to be *good*. I am called to be *great*. I had to get comfortable once again with being uncomfortable. I'd been experiencing pain in my heart. I realized they were growing pains.

With our whole heart, we are to seek, find, and eventually grow. Submitting all our fleshly desires to rise above the cares of this world, we are called to soar above. Too many times we allow the circumstances and storms of our lives to hinder our growth.

We think and say the usual things: "It's too hard." "No one has it as bad." "It's not worth the effort." Growth can be painful; change can be painful. But nothing is as painful as staying stuck where we don't belong.

Devotion, Day 10

Lord Jesus, I desire to go to a new level in You. Help me to rise up and drop the excuses. To go the extra mile, I must dedicate more of myself to You. When I go off course, convict me by the power of your Spirit. I choose today to surrender and submit no matter how painful it may be. With my whole heart, I seek You, Lord. In Jesus's name, Amen.

Reflections

*"Those who hope in the Lord will renew their
strength. They will soar on wings like eagles"*

Isaiah 40:31, NIV

Day 11

*"That their hearts may be encouraged,
having been knit together in love, and
attaining to all the wealth that comes
from the full assurance of understanding,
resulting in a true knowledge of God's
mystery, that is, Christ Himself"*

Col 2:2

I had a close relationship with my mother-in-law Mary. While visiting my in-laws in Decatur, Alabama, she and I would sit for hours on Saturday mornings as we sipped on coffee, read devotions, and talked about deep spiritual matters, including the mystery of Christ. Those Saturday morning talks hugely shaped me by impacting the early years in my faith.

My father-in-law, at one point, started an outreach that involved rising early on Sunday mornings and driving a bus, provided by the church, to a local trailer park, where he would pick up children and take them to church services. It was a different time, and parents trusted him, so they'd send their children out to the bus to go with Mr. Teague. I went with him once, and it touched me deeply to see the kids run up to the bus, so excited for the opportunity to attend church. Even more touching, bringing tears to my eyes, one of the kids accepted Christ on that Sunday.

One Saturday afternoon, Mary got out an old devotional book of hers—*Meditations for Men* by Daniel Russell—to share a story with me about two men who helped homeless people at settlement houses. (Shelters were referred to as *settlement houses* at the time the book was published, in 1955.) One of the men serving gave little thought to God, and he was shocked that his efforts were not appreciated. Growing cynical, he decided the underprivileged deserved nothing and quit.

The other man, profoundly religious, walked in the mystical presence of the Divine. He saw in every brother a special soul for whom Christ died. He remembered that a rejected Christ nevertheless dominates the hearts of men. He knew that success should be secondary; doing the will of Christ and leaving the results to Him were primary. Instead of growing cynical, he mellowed. Though his work was hidden from the eyes of men, he was born and carried others with him on the bosom of a heroic faith and an unwavering love. This man lived in the spirit of the Word. The other did not.

That devotion stuck with me. The story, along with the trailer park outreach, which made the children so happy about coming to church, plus the long talks with Mary had a combined effect. The Mystery of Christ followed me back to Atlanta, and, as mentioned, I was eventually called to birth Victoria's Friends, a sex-trafficking ministry.

When we operate in the mystery of Christ, we see everything with spiritual eyes. It's like first watching a movie in 2D and then seeing it again in 3D. Wow! The colors and details suddenly pop off the screen.

May we follow that Mystery of Christ in our endeavors and stay in 3D as we reach out to a hurting world.

Devotion, Day 11

Lord Jesus, help me today to reach out in love in the Mystery of Christ. I know that when I reach out in my flesh, bitterness, resentment, and a cynical attitude come over me. Help me to stay in my 3D flow with the Mystery of Christ in all I put my hands and heart, too! In Jesus's name, Amen.

Reflections

*"Praise be to the God and Father of our Lord
Jesus Christ, the Father of compassion and the
God of all comfort, who comforts us in all our
troubles, so that we can comfort those in any
trouble with the comfort we ourselves
receive from God"*

2 Corinthians 1:3-4

Day 12

"But who am I, and who are my people, that we should be able to give as generously as this? Everything comes from you, and we have given you only what comes from your hand"

1 Chronicles 29:14

One of the saddest days for the Victoria's Friends' ministry team arrived when a dear friend of ours received a phone call that his eighteen-year-old son had passed away while he was on the way to bury his mother. The news was totally unexpected.

How would any of us process a moment of heading to one funeral and finding out we had another huge loss? Only by God's grace and His hand on it can we get through that day.

We quickly gathered our thoughts and offered to help our friend. His request for us was a beautiful one. He simply wanted twelve dozen rose petals spread around his son's gravesite, but we were in the middle of the world pandemic of COVID-19. Everything was closing down as Georgia was sheltering in.

We locked down the roses with the local farmer's market only to find out they'd already closed by the time we went to purchase the petals. A volunteer with Victoria's Friends just happened to notice a florist sign on the way back from the market. Assuming they'd be closed with the rest of the world, he nevertheless pulled into the florist's parking lot and rang the doorbell. To my volunteer's surprise, a sweet man in his seventies came to the door.

It's amazing how God coordinates situations. The florist poured out his heart. Times had been hard, and he was about to lose his shop. My volunteer explained how desperate we were to get the petals, the only request from our dear friend, and it just so happened that the florist had roses of all colors. Delighted to help, he pulled off the petals and placed them in boxes for us. It was a double blessing because we were able to give him a gift card and some food items that were difficult to find.

My friend's son's graveside service was so special, and my heart swelled as we scattered the petals. We had to follow the restrictions about keeping our distance from one another for the service, so we staggered people up on a hillside with everyone standing six feet apart. The most beautiful spirit of the Lord came over us all as we sang and celebrated my friend's son. The rose petals and additional flowers the florist made for us were miracles during COVID-19.

A few days later, I headed out for my predictable morning hike. My daughter, home from college, joined me. We took off down a trail that was familiar to us, yet for some reason Hannah noticed an offshoot path that veered to the right. We decided to take it.

I was asking how we'd never noticed that trail before, and we decided it must have been covered with leaves. We headed down a tight slope before reaching a wider path. At some point, looking down at my feet, I noticed a line of little flowers. They were rimmed in gold and shaped like miniature trumpets. We continued to walk and talk, and when I looked down again, white flower petals were covering the path. I pointed out to Hannah how beautiful they were. I had never before noticed flower petals on our trail. Pink ones appeared next. Before the day was over, we encountered a massive carpet of flowers and petals. It was a sheer delight with all the varieties combined.

Finally, I caught on, paused, and prayed. *God, this is you?* I recognized His thumbprint. God had colored our new trail! We had blessed our dear friend with the rose petals, and God was blessing us. It was a beautiful hike, and what a beautiful treat!

Two days later, I returned to the same trail for the same hike, and there were no flowers, no petals. Whoa!

Clearly, during that time of grieving over my friend's son's death, God had showed up—bigtime!

Moral of the story: We cannot out-give God! He'll just keep blessing us and blessing us.

What an amazing sense of joy to see God out-give us, every single time. When we bless other people, God will bless us more than we could possibly imagine. I want us all to have that same joy.

Here's some food for thought:

> When have we seen God bless us after we've chosen to be generous?

> Did joy come from giving? If not, what prevented us from feeling happy?

> What kind of commitment to giving can we make that will stretch our faith as we keep it?

Devotion, Day 12

Lord Jesus, help us to be generous in all that we do. Help us to share our time, our treasures, and our talents. As we do, we know that You will show up and show out! I thank You, God, for Your generosity and know we can never out-give You!

"I will make you rich in every way"

2 Corinthians 9:11

Reflections

*"Remember this: Whoever sows sparingly will
also reap sparingly, and whoever sows generously
will also reap generously. Each of you should give
what you have decided in your heart to give, not
reluctantly or under compulsion, for God
loves a cheerful giver"*

2 Corinthians 9:6-8

_____
_____
_____
_____
_____
_____
_____
_____
_____
_____
_____
_____
_____
_____
_____
_____
_____
_____

Last Call

> *"Godly men are growing a tree that bears*
> *life-giving fruit, and all who win*
> *souls are wise"*

Proverbs 11:30

In closing out this devotional, I want to share a story.

Years ago, I worked late hours in the club scene as a dancer. As the early morning hours would pour in, the bartender would flip on the lights and say, "Last call. Last call for alcohol!" I would always have that one customer who would try to slip the bartender an extra twenty dollars to get another drink. Sometimes the bartender would agree to do it.

Writing this in the season of a world pandemic, I wonder if we are truly on a last call.

I was sharing that thought with a dear family friend. He has been wonderful to my daughter and helped me with several projects. A very fine young man with a strong work ethic, he's definitely the type my husband and I would want to marry our daughter. Yet, he has never made a commitment for Christ. We have discussed it at length. He says, "It's fine for you, Moms V.," addressing me the way many of the kids do, "but it has to be right for me."

I've asked him, "What would it take for it to be right for you?" He typically responds with crickets. He doesn't have an answer. Recently, he said, "I'm young. I have time."

I truly hope that we all have time to make a decision for Christ, but what if we are on last call?

The Word says, "Thousands upon thousands are waiting in the valley of decision. There the day of the LORD will soon arrive" (Joel 3:14).

For those among us who stand in the valley of decision, it is time to make a decision for Christ. The Word says all who win souls are wise. It is the best decision to make. There's no deeper treasure than to be in Christ and to win souls for Christ.

When we find the love of Jesus Christ, walking through the purging and refining process, discovering who we are in Christ (the answer is *royalty*), we must go out and share with the world.

*"Therefore, go and make disciples of all nations,
baptizing them in the name of the Father and of
the Son and of the Holy Spirit … and teaching
them to obey everything I have commanded you.
And surely, I am with you always, to the
very end of the age"*

Matthew 28:18-20

God is for you, He is with you, and He loves you!

From the Heart of Victoria

*F*rom the bits and pieces of my story, you've gathered that many years ago I found myself in a difficult place. Sexually abused in childhood and raped at sixteen years of age led to my involvement with the wrong crowd. Bankrupt from drugs and poor life choices, I ended up homeless. I then met an amazing woman of God named Pam Younker, and I will forever be grateful to her. Pam and her family took me into their home and loved, adored, and cherished me. Through my season with this special family, I too began to feel special. I realized that something bigger than I brought me to this place of love. Through Pam's guidance and tender, loving care, I realized a God of the Universe existed and that He had carried me this far.

The Reverend Billy Graham often told a story of a turtle on a fence post that couldn't have gotten there on his own. I was also helplessly crawling on the ground like a turtle until someone lifted me up. I went from barely surviving in a drug house to living in an upper-middle class home overnight. I never would have gotten there without God's grace and intervention. I would have had no way of arriving at the place I am today without God's grace and intervention. Only God can orchestrate something like that. I should have died out on the streets, yet God, in His grace and mercy, brought Pam to take me in and care for me.

I found a place where I felt forever safe, forever accepted, forever held, completely loved, and always wanted. That place is with Jesus!

No matter our social class, race, background, religion, or anything else favorable or unfavorable in the eyes of men, we are children of God. He desires and longs for us to come into His family. All we have to say is, *Jesus, remember me.* He will come and take a place in our heart and fill our cup with the most irresistible love. As we fill up on this love, we become bright lights in this world!

Let your lights shine brightly!

All of my love,
Victoria

For more information on the stories shared or Victoria's Friends, please visit www.victorias-friends.com.

> *"I have come that they may have life,*
> *and have it to the full"*

John 10:10

On the night that Christ died, He suffered torment; hung in the shame of nakedness; was beaten, torn and twisted until he could no longer bear it. He died on the cross of redemption so that we could trade our rebellion for repentance.

The men hanging on either side of Jesus at Calvary had the same choice. While one took his bitterness and rage to the grave, the other cried out, "Remember me!"

Jesus doesn't hold our past against us. He took our shame, our guilt, our bruises and iniquities so that we could live free from their grip!

We will face trials. We will face attacks. We will suffer in this fallen world. But we cannot let the enemy keep us from our destiny.

What will you do with this man in the middle of the three crosses? His name is Jesus Christ of Nazareth. Will you be like the thief, hanging on the cross next to Jesus, and say, "Remember me, Jesus. Remember me."?

If you have made this exciting leap of faith with Jesus and would like more information, please contact Victoria's Friends through our website, www.Victorias-Friends.com, or by calling us at 678-218-7188.

Welcome to the family of God!